CHRISTIANBURG CHURCH MINUTES

1822–1872

MONROE COUNTY
TENNESSEE

W.P.A. Records

Heritage Books
2024

HERITAGE BOOKS

AN IMPRINT OF HERITAGE BOOKS, INC.

Books, CDs, and more—Worldwide

For our listing of thousands of titles see our website
at
www.HeritageBooks.com

A Facsimile Reprint
Published 2024 by
HERITAGE BOOKS, INC.
Publishing Division
5810 Ruatan Street
Berwyn Heights, MD 20740

September 15, 1938

International Standard Book Number
Paperbound: 978-0-7884-8810-8

WPA RECORDS

The WPA Records are, for the most part, carbon copies of the original that was typed on onion skin paper during the Depression. Since these records were typed on poor machines by people who did not type well either and read by persons not always sure of the older handwritten material, the results are often less that perfect.

We have made every attempt to make as good a copy as can be made from these older papers. Sometimes there are water stains and burned edges around the paper.. This is the results of a fire at the home of one of the workers, Mrs. Penelope Allen, who was over most of the project.

The WPA Records are now very scattered between the State Archives, various Public and Private Libraries and other collections. Some day, there is a hope that all of these can be collected and stored in one place. In spite of their many mistakes and problems, these are still the most complete collection of Tennessee records found anywhere.

MONROE COUNTY

CHRISTIANBURG CHURCH MINUTES
1828-1872

VOL. I

NEW INDEX

Note: Page numbers in this index refer to those of the original volume from which this copy was made. These numbers are
inserted within parentheses throughout the text, as (p 124).

F (Cont.)

Forkner, Joseph, 121, 122
Fortner, G. J., 116
Fortner, James G., 102
Foshee, M., 100
Four Mile, 58, 59
Frisby, Bayts, 73
Friendship, 63, 65
Frisby, July Ann, 68
Frisby, Luke, 73
Fry, John, 2, 5
Fry, Katharine, 5

G

Gallaher, John, 115
Gan, Anna, 49
Gan, Henry, 49, 54
Gan, T. H., 55
Gill, C., 88
Gill, Curtis, 74, 88, 91
Gill, Jain, 73
Givens, Elder, 24, 26
Givens, John, 19, 50, 61
Golden, John, 3, 4
Goodfield, 48, 57, 63, 65
Goodfield Church, 61, 75, 76
Grayson, Albert, 73
Gun, A., 93
Gun, Catherine, 93

H

Hambrick, 100
Hambrick, Caroline, 104
Hambrick, J., 104
Hambrick, James, 104
Harden, Margaret, 18
Harden, Moss, 18
Harden, William, 5, 8
Hardin, Adline, 21, 23
Hare, Wm., 81
Hares, E. F., 125
Haris, Salinei, 120
Hariss, E. F., 125
Harmon, 22, 74
Harmon, Milley, 76
Harmon, Nancy, 76
Harmon, Rachel, 22, 5, 8
Harrell, Hazel, 73, 82
Harrell, M. C., 74
Harrell, Mary Jain, 23, 36
Harrell, Nancy, 23
Harrell, Robert, 100
Harrell, Sally, 28
Harrell, Thomas, 74

Harrill, A., 117, 125
Harrill, Aaron, 116
Harrill, Francis, 105
Harrill, Katharine, 29
Harrill, May Jain, 29
Harrill, Robert, 109
Harress, Caroline, 119
Harriette, (black) 81
Harris, Sally E., 123
Harris, Thomas G., 123
Hartley, Benjamin, 71
Hartley, Matilda, 71
Haun, A., 104, 105, 107, 111, 112
Haun, Abraham, 32, 43, 54
Haun, Absolom, 38
Haun, E. N., 119
Haun, Elen, 112
Haun, Ellen, 104
Haun, Jain, 57
Haun, S., 57
Haun, S. M., 62, 71, 82, 85, 86, 90, 99, 100, 103, 109, 113, 116, 117, 118, 120, 121, 124, 126
Haun, Samuel, 57
Haun, Samuel M., 79
Hawarton, John, 3
Henderson, Mary Ann, 52
Henderson, Polly Ann, 39
Hensley, E., 75
Hensley, C. L., 83, 93
Herd, E. C., 93, 102
Herd, James M., 100
Herd, Mary, 93
Herrell, Catharine, 67, 78
Herrell, Frank, 100
Herrell, H. W., 74, 98
Herrell, Margaret, 100
Herrell, Matilda, 90
Herrell, Sarah, 65
Herrell, Thomas, 102
Herrill, George, 92
Herrill, Hazel, 73
Herrill, Sarah Isabel, 93
Herrill, T. C., 90
Herrold, Katharine, 12
Herrold, Nancy, 12
Herrold, Sarah, 12
Hickman, 75
Hickman, Sister, 76
Hicks, Mammrvy, 18
Hicks, Susan, 116
Higgans, Jiney, 12

W (Cont.)

Walker, Nancy, 32, 49
Walker, Sally Jain, 32
Walker, Seth, 39, 51, 68
Wallis, Gavin, 88
Wallis, Thos., 44, 48, 63
Wallis, Thomas, 38, 103
Wallis, Wm., 26
Warrack, Samuel, 52, 55, 57
Warric, Katharine, 37
Warric, Nancy, 37
Warric, Elizabeth, 87
Warrick, Katharine, 49
Warrick, Margaret, 87
Warrick, Mary, 87
Warrick, Nancy, 73, 74, 97
Warrick, Samuel, 49, 50, 52, 54
Warrick, Williams, 64
Warrick, Wm., 67
Watson, William, 55
Watson, Wm., 41
Watson, Mary Jane, 12
Weathers, James, 73, 116
Weathers, Sarah, 100
Weathers, Sarah Caroline, 71
Weathers, Wilson, 73
Webb, R. A., 90
West, Bartlett, 73
West, Elizabeth, 111, 115
West, Mary, 71
West, Mary Ann, 82
West, Matilda, 93
West, Sarah, 111

W (Cont.)

West, Savannah, 11
West, Susannah, 17
White, Mary, 87
William, S. E., 100
Williams, Elizabeth, 91, 122
Williams, G. I., 102
Williams, George, 39, 51, 54, 55, 58, 103
Williams, Jacob, 76, 88, 103
Williams, Jeramarah, 106
Williams, Jeremiah, 90
Williams, Mary, 93
Williams, Nancy, 93, 102, 105
Williams, S., 90
Williams, Samuel, 66, 67
Williams, Sara, 105
Williams, Sarah, 84
Willis, (black) 12, 19
Willis, Brother, 33
Willmouth, Rachel, 12, 23

Y

Young McMinn Church, 122

Z

Zion Hill, 18

FINIS

P-1   RULS OF DECORUM

1st   the Church shall be opened And Closed by prayer

2nd   One person only shall speak at the same time Who shall rise from
their seat And address the Moderator when they Are About to make a speach

3rd   the person speaking shal not be interrupted by Any person except the
Moderator until they are done speaking

4th   the person speaking shall strictly Adher to the subject under Consideration And shall in no wise either reflect on Or make any unfrinly
remarks on the imperfections of the person who speaks before them but
shall fairly state the Case an Convey there ideas on the subject as
Casiesly as posible.

5th   No member of Church shall absent themself from the Church Without
leave from the Moderator

6th.   No person shall speak more than three times on Any one subject without leave from the Church

7th   No member or other person shall have liberty of Whispering or Laugh-
fing During time of publick Worship in the Church

8th   No member of the Church shall Address Another in Any other Appella-
tion then that of Brother or Sister

9th   The Moderator shall not interrupt Any member of the Church When speaking untill they are done speaking or give there light on the subject un-
less they should violate the Rules of the Church

10th   Any member of the Church who shall Knowlingly violate any of the
Rules of the Church shall be reproved by the Church as may be thought
proper.

the above rules for the government of the Church were Red and Received
And Signed By the Moderator and Cleark May 2nd Saturday 1840.

                                        Thomas Stephens, Clerk

P-2   FIRST SATURDAY IN JANUARY 1829 -

the Church met And After Worship opened A door for the Reception of mem-

bers. Brother John Fry Requested a letter Brother John Howarton And
Wife which Was granted.

P-3

THE FIRST SATURDAY IN FEBRUARY A. D. 1828.

The arm of Sweetwater Church met and after Divine Worship opened a Door
for the Reception of Members & Received Thomas Stephens By Experience,
then named our Meeting house Christianburg.

> John Tendal, Mod.
> John Laws, C. C.

FIRST SATURDAY MARCH 1828

The Church met and After Divine Worship opened a door for the Reception
of Members & Received James McNabb & Nancy his Wife And Polly his daughter
& Levi B. Hunt by letter. Received George McNabb & Susannah Norman by
Experience then Appointed Brother Levi B. Hunt Church Clerk And Tolerated him to preach The Gospel in the Bounds of the Church.

FIRST SATURDAY IN MAY 1828

The Church met And after Divine Worship opened a door for the Reception
of Members & C.

FIRST SATURDAY IN JUEN 1828 -

the Church met And after Worship opened a Door for the Reception of Members

Received James Laws, John Hawarton & wife, John Golden, Emilia Norman
and Reay Larrymore by letter & John Norman by Experience &c.

> Levi B. Hunt   C. C.

FIRST SATURDAY IN JULY 1828

The Church Met And after Worship opened a Door for the Reception of Mem-
bers, then Chose Brother George Stephens Deacon for this Church then
Agreed to have a Communion Season to Commence the Fryday before the first
Saturday September &c.

> Levi B. Hunt   C. C.

FIRST SATURDAY IN AUGUST 1828.

The Church met and After Worship opened a Door And Received John Fry by
Experience Saturday after Worship opened a Door then Tolerated Brother
Levi B. Hunt To preach the Gospel Wherever God in his providence may
Cast his lot - then Appoint Brother Levi B. Hunt to be Our Deligate to
Represent us in the ensuing Association at Pisga Meeting house Saturday,
the Church, after Worship, proceeded to Business And took a Charge Against
Elyah Laws that of Fornication for which the Church declared an unfellow-
ship with him

P-4   FIRST SATURDAY OCTOBER 1828.

the Church met and after Divine Worship opened a Door then Brought a
charge against Sarah Renfrow Even that of Fornication for Which the Church
declared an unfellowship With her - - - -Brother John Golden petition a
letter Which Was granted.

FIRST SATURDAY IN NOV. 1828.

The Church Met and after Worship opened a door for the Reception of Members the Church petition her Mother Church at Sweetwater for dismission
in order to become a Constituted Church and that she should Chose a presbytry to Attend us on fryday before the first Saturday in December for the
purpose of setting us apart and allso to Ordain our Deacns - -

FIRST SATURDAY DEC.

the Church Met and After Worship Opened a Door for the Reception of Members - - -

Renew a petition to her Mother Church Fryday before the first Saturday in
Feb. 1829 - - - And after worship opened a Door -

Saturday the Church met and proceeded to business after worship And pe-
titioned Sweetwater, Pond Creek, Chestua, and Tellico for their Ministerial help to attend us the fryday before the first Saturday in April -

FIRST SATURDAY IN MARCH 1829.

The Church met and After Worship opened A Door Brother Elisha Laws Request A letter for himself, Wife and sister Which Was Granted.

Fryday before the first Saturday in April 1829. The Church
met and After Worship opened a door.

Saturday the Church proceeded to business. Choose Brethern Elder Eli Cleveland, William Jones & Jayson Mattlock for a presbytry who set us Apart by prayer as A free and independant United Baptist Church of Christ on the following Abstract of ~~preambles~~. principles

1st. We believe in one, only true and living God, the father, Son and Holy Ghost and these three Are one

2nd. We believe that the Scriptures of the old and new testament is the word of God and the only Rule of All Saving Knowledge.

3rd. We believe in Election according to the fore-knowledge of God the Father through the Sanctification of the Spirits.

4th. We believe in the Doctrine of Original Sin

P-5   5th. We believe in Man's impotency to Recover himself from the fall or state he is in by his own free will ability -

6th. We believe that Sinners is justified in the light of God only by the imputed Righteousness Jesus Christ.

7th. We believe that Saints Will persevier in Grace and never finally fall away

8th. We believe that Baptism And the Lord's Supper Are ordinances of Jesus Christ And true Believers is the only Subjects of these Ordinances And the only true mode of Baptism is by immersion.

9th. We believe that the Resurrection of the dead and a General Judgment - -

10th. We believe that the punishment of the Wicked Will be everlasting and the joys of the Righteous Eternal.

11th. We believe that no Minister has a right to the Administration of the ordinances only such as Are regularly Called And Come under the hands by a presbytery . . ..

Levi B. Hunt	Nancy McNabb
John Howarton	Polly McNabb
George Stephens	Reay Larrymore
James Laws	Nancy Clark
James McNabb	Winney Renfrow
Thomas Stephens	Nancy Clark
John Norman	Emilia Norman
William Harden	Polly Stephens
John Fry	Susannah Norman
George McNabb	Patsy Renfrow
Andrew McNabb	Katharine Fry

the Church Met and After Worship opened a door for the Reception of Members

2nd Brother James McNabb, Nancy and Polly McNabb petition letters and was granted.

FIRST SATURDAY IN JUNE

the Church met and After Worship Opened a Door for the Reception of Members, than A petition the Ministerial helps from Sweetwater, Tellico and Big Springs Churches to attend us on the Fryday before the First Saturday in August

Fryday before the first Saturday in August 1829 the Church met And After divine Worship opened a door for the reception of Members " "

the Church met on Saturday Appointed Levi B. Hunt, Church Clerk to Write a letter to the Association to Convene At Shilow Meeting house. Allso received Daniel B. Hopkins by letter allso Chose Brother George Stephens to the office of Deacon and set him apart for Ordination then Choose Brethern Elders Eli Cleveland and Daniel Buckner As after Presbytry who set him Apart by prayer And the laying on of his hands.

THE FIRST SATURDAY IN SEPTEMBER 1829

the Church met And After divine Worship opened a door for the receiption of Members

FIRST SATURDAY IN OCTOBER 1829

The Church met And after Divine Worship opened a door for the Receiption of Members. Agreed to have a Church Meeting on fryday before the third Saturday of this month. The church mt on the time above Appointed.

P-7   FIRST SATURDAY IN DECEMBER 1829

The Church met and After Divine Worship opened A door for the Reception of Members . . . .

FIRST SATURDAY IN JANUARY 1830

the Church met And After Divine Worship opened a Door for the Reception of Members.

THE FIRST SATURDAY IN FEBRUARY 1830

the Church met and after Divine Worship opened a Door for the Reception of Members

THE FIRST SATURDAY IN MARCH 1830.

The Church Met And after Publick Worship opened a Door .. .&C

THE FIRST SATURDAY IN APRIEL 1830

The Church met and after Worship opened a Door for the Reception of Members

FIRST SATURDAY IN JULY 1830

The Church Met And after Divine Worship opened a Door for the Reception of Members

FIRST SATURDAY IN AUGUST 1830.

The Church Met and After Worship opened a door . .

Sister Recey Brought a Charge Against Sister Winney Renfrow for keeping a disorderly house for which the Church declared an unfellowship with her, believing the Charge to be true.

The Church Appoint Brethern Levi B. Hunt an Daniel Hopkins deligates to the Hiwassee Association. Elijah Laws pray the Church to Reconsider his exclusion which Was Granted And him restored to Fellowship in the Church.

FIRST SATURDAY IN OCTOBER 1830

the Church met and after Worship opened a door

the Church Appoint Brethern Levi B. Hunt and George Stephens to represent us in the Convention to be held at Brother Eli Clevelands on the 4th Saturday in Nov. Also appoint Brother Levi B. Hunt to write our letter to the Convention.

P-8   FIRST SATURDAY IN NOVEMBER 1830

The Church Met and After Worship opened a door.

Brother Daniel Hopkins Request a letter And it Was granted
Brother Elijah Laws petition a letter which was granted.
Brother William Hardin petition a letter and was granted

FIRST SATURDAY IN DECEMBER 1830

The Church met and after Worship opened a door - -

FIRST SATURDAY IN JANUARY 1831

the Church met and after Worship opened a door

Brother John Norman petition a letter for himself, Wife &
daughter Susannah which Was Granted.

FIRST SATURDAY IN FEB.

the Church opened a door &C.

FIRST SATURDAY IN MARCH, 1831

the Church met and After Worship opened a door for the Reception
of Members

FIRST SATURDAY IN APRIL 1831

the Church met and after Worship opened a door.

FIRST SATURDAY IN MAY 1831

the Church met opened a door -

FIRST SATURDAY IN JUNE 1831

The Church met and after Worship opened a door.

FIRST SATURDAY IN JULY 1831

the Church Met and After Divine Worship opened a Door for the Reception of Members. Then took up the following Query

is it agreeable to Gospel Order to hold a Member in fellowship who hath not Wherewith to support himself and family and will not use the necessary Means by industry for their support And agreed to refer it to the Association

then agreed to petition for Ministerial help to attend us the fryday before the first Saturday in August next in order to administer the Lord's Supper then Appoint Brother Levi B. Hunt to Write a letter to the Association And Chose Brethern Levi B. Hunt deligate to the Association

FIRST SATURDAY IN AUGUST 1831

the Church Met and after Worship opened a door for the reception of Members.

FIRST SATURDAY IN SEPTEMBER 1831

the Church met and opened a door

FIRST SATURDAY IN OCTOBER 1831

the Church met and opened a door for the Reception of Members.

FIRST SATURDAY IN NOV.

the Church met and opened a door - - -

P-9
FIRST SATURDAY IN DECEMBER

The church met and after worship opened a door etc.

FIRST SATURDAY IN JANUARY 1832

the Church met and after worship opened a door for Received Nancy Hurst by experience

P-10   FIRST SATURDAY JULY 1832

the Church met And After Divine Worship opened a Door - -

FIRST SATURDAY IN AUGUST 1832

the Church met and After Worship opened a door for the Reception of Members. then appointed Brother Levi B. Hunt And George Stephens Delligates to Represent us in the Association.

SEPTEMBER 1832.

the Church Met And after Worship opened A door - - -

FIRST SATURDAY OCTOBER 1832

the Church met and after Worship opened a door and received by experience Solomon Seviney - then agreed to petition Ministerial help to attend us on the fryday before the first Saturday in December next in Order to set apart Brother Levi B. Hunt to the Ministry by Ordination.

Then declared an unfellowship With Patsy Reanfrow on an Acknowledgement she made of being guilty of unchristian Conduct even by Fornication.

FOURTH SATURDAY OCTOBER 1832.

The Church Met and after worship opened a door and Received Elizabeth Cunningham, Ruth Fergerson, and Caroline Celena Hunt by experience and Elenar Mellon by letter

FRYDAY BEFORE THE FIRST SATURDAY IN DECEMBER 1832

the Church met and after Worship opened a door then Appoint Brethern Levi B. Hunt and Brothers George Stephens to attend at fork
Creek to know of the Brethern if they will aprobate our moving Our meeting house And Agreed to hold meeting at Brother Stephens until we build a new meetinghouse.

Saturday the Church Met And After Worship Choose Brethern Elders Eli Cleveland Richard Talliferre John Selvidge and Jayson Mattlock to be our Presbytery who proceed in the examination of Brother Levi B. Hunt on his Call to the Ministry and believing him to be orthodox in

Sentiment and Doctrine Set him Apart to preach the Gospel by prayer and laying on of the hands Done By order of the Whole Church the first Saturday in December 1832 Saturday evening.

Brother Andrew McNabb Request a letter Which Was granted Sabbath morning after Worship opened a door Received a black woman called Rachel and Thomas Reanfrow by Experience.

P-11   Then John Crisp solicited the Church to receive him under her Watch-care stating that he once belonged to the Baptist Church in Chester District in South Carolina but had been excluded.After hearing his Recantation the Church took him in their care until she Could Write to the Church to which he said he once belonged And Appointed Brother Levi B. Hunt to Write a letter to that Church

Tuesday the Church met and after worship opened a door for the Reception of Members and Received John Carter by experience. . . .

FIRST SATURDAY JANUARY 1833.

the Church met and opened a door and received Nancy Caps by experience.

FIRST SATURDAY IN FEBRUARY 1833

the Church met i opened a door and received Matilda Rickets by letter . . . .

FIRST SATURDAY IN APRIEL

the Church met and After Worship opened a door and received Elizabeth Walker by letter

then brought a Charge against Brother James Laws for Sabbath Breaking it was laid over until next meeting met at Candle Light

then received Polly Hightower by experience.

FIRST SATURDAY IN MAY 1833

the Church met and after worship opened a Door

received Savannah West by experience,

then took up the Charge against John Crisp and declared an unfellowship with him

then took up the Charge Against brother James Laws And After hearing his acknowledgement forgave him

FIRST SATURDAY IN MARCH 1833

the Church met and opened a door and received Patsy Cunningham by experience

then received Ruth Sumey by letter

FIRST SATURDAY IN JUNE 1833

the Church met and After Worship opened a door and received Lavina Horton by letter.

FIRST SATURDAY IN JULY 1833 -

the Church met and after Worship Agreed to petition Ministerial help to Attend us on the fryday before the first_____Saturday in September to Administer the Lord's Supper and also to ordain Brother Solomon Sumey to the office of a Deacon -

then Appointed Brother Thomas Stephens Assistant Clerk

Sabbath the Church met and After Worship Received Simeon Dilda and Wife by letter

FIRST SATURDAY IN AUGUST 1833

the Church met And After Worship opened a door . . .

then Appointed Brother Levi B. Hunt to Write a letter to the Association and then Appointed Brethern Levi B. Hunt and Solomon Sumey Deligates to the same

P-12   Then Appointed Brethern Solomon Sumey George Stephen and Job Carter Trustees of Our Meeting house and place of Worship.

Then the Church brought a Charge Against Brother James Laws for executing a note in another man's name and allso for bringing a suit in the same man's name on an order as agent for him without leave and after hearing him and the testimony Against him declared an unfellowship with him.

Sabbath the Church opened a door and received Polly Prestwood her Son and Daughter Leandrew and Elizabeth by experience.

FRYDAY BEFORE THE FIRST SATURDAY IN SEPTEMBER 1833

the Church Met and After Worship opened a door for the Reception of Members

Saturday Met and After Worship Received Absolom Prestwood by experience. Received Martha Cunningham an Jacob Page by experience & Elias Dilda and Wife by letter

then Chose a Presbytry to Wit Brethern Elders Robert Snead Jayson Mattlock and Levi B. Hunt to set Brother Solomon Sumey apart to the office of a Deacon which they done by prayer and the laying on of hands –

Saturday evening Met And After Worship opened a door and Received a man of Colour by the name of Willis.

Saturday Morning After Worship opened a door

Monday the Church met, opened her door.

Tuesday the Church Met and after Worship opened a door and received Zelph Christian by experience and Jeremiah Cunningham by letter

Tuesday evening received William Higgans and Wife Jiney and Sarah Barnett and Sarah Herrold by experience.

Wednesday morning the Church met and after Worship opened a door for the Reception of Members Received Drady Ray, Caroline Walker and Ealenor Christian by experience.

Wednesday evening the Church met and after worship received a Young man of Colour by the name of James, Sarah Newland and Mary Jane Walton by experience.

The Church met on Monday evening the 16th and after Worship opened a door for the reception of Members and received Nancy and Katherine Herrold, Polly Ann, Ferguson, George Christian and William Ray by experience

Tuesday Morning the Church Met And After Worship opened a Door

FIRST SATURDAY IN OCTOBER

the Church met and after Worship opened a door and Received Elenor Blades by Experience then Adjourned until Evening.

Met and received by Experience Preston G. B. Melton, Rachel Willmouth and Judy Ray.

FIRST SATURDAY NOVEMBER 1833

The Church met And   (P-13)   After Worship received a woman of collor by the name of Abie by experience.

FIRST SATURDAY IN DECEMBER 1833

the Church met and opened a Dore then adjourned

FIRST SATURDAY IN JANUARY 1834

the Church Met and After Worship opened a dore for the Reception the Church Agreed to send for Brother George McNabb and appointed Brother George Stephens and Solomon Sumey to bring him to the Church by next Meeting. the Brother George Stephens Applied for leter of Dishmission for a Woman of Color And Was Granted by the Name of Rachel.

FIRST SATURDAY IN FEBRUARY 1834

the Church met and After Worship took up the Case of Brother George McNabb and layed it over

FIRST SATURDAY MARCH 1834

Church met and After Worship Brother George McNabb came forward to the Church and paid an acknowledgement and the Church forgave him then adjourned, met Coming After Worship opened a dore forthe reception of members and Received by Experience Patsy Melton

FIRST SATURDAY MAY 1834

Church met and after Worship opened a dore for the Reception of Members then Dismissed by leter Levi B. Hunt Wife Nancy and Daughter Caroline, Celena Polly Hitower, Elias Dilda and Wife, Simeon Dilda and Wife Marthy

the the Church Appointed Brother Thomas Stephens their Church Clark.

Thomas Stephens   C. C.

FIRST SATURDAY IN JUNE 1834

Church Met and After Worship opened a dore for the reception of Members.

Church agreed to pertishion Mt. Pleasant, Tellice, Sweetwater, & Prospect for their Ministerial helps to Attend us on Friday before the first Saturday in September next in order to preach the Word and to Administer the Lord's Supper on Sabbath and Appointed Brother Thos. Stephens Solomon Sumey & John Carter to bare said pertishions.

Thomas Stephens   C. C.

FIRST SATURDAY JULY 1834

Church met And After Worship opened and adjourned

FIRST SATURDAY AUGUST 1834

Church Met And After Worship opened a dore for the Reception of Members

then the Church Agreed to have a leter Wrote and brought to our next meeting for inspection to send to the Association and Appointed Thomas Stephens

P-14   Received by Experience Anna Cunningham Andrew McNabb

William Higgens & Jerrymiah Cunningham as Deligates to the Association then Adjourned

Met evening opened a dore for the reception of Members And received by Experience Anna Cunningham and Andrew McNabb then Adjourned.

Thos Stephens   C. C.

FRIDAY BEFORE THE FIRST SATURDAY IN SEPT. 1834

the Church Met and After Worship opened a Dore for the Reception of Members   then Adjourned.

Met Saturday After Worship Adjourned

Met Sabbath morning After Worship adjourned

Met a Monday after Worship then the Clerk took up the Charge

against Nancy Capps for joining the Methodist Society, and after hearing
from her Declares an unfellowship With her then Adjourned.

Met Tuesday morning after Worship opened and Adjourned.

Thomas Stephens C.C.

FIRST SATURDAY IN NOVEMBER 1834

Church met and opened her Dors and Adjourned.

Thomas Stephens C. C.

FIRST SATURDAY IN DECEMBER 1834

Church met an after worship opened her Dors for the reception
of members &c.

Thomas Stephens C.C.

FIRST SATURDAY IN JANUARY 1834

the Church met and after Divine Worship opened her dors for the
receptions of Members and adjourns until Sabbath

Met and after worship opened her dors for the Reception of Members and received Bartlet Renfrow by Letter and dismissed George McNabb
By letter Done by order of the Church the day above Written

Thomas Stephens C. C.

FIRST SATURDAY IN MARCH 1835.

Church met and After Divine Worship opened her dors for the
reception of Members &c.

FIRST SATURDAY IN APRIEL 1835.

the Church met and after divine Worship (P-15) opened her
dors for the Reception of Members &c. First the Church brought in Charges
Against Ealenar Christian for not attending the meeting for which the
Church declares an unfellowship Against her. Done by order of the Church

Thomas Stephens C.C.

FIRST SATURDAY IN MAY 1835

the Church met and After Divine Worship opened a dore for the Reception of Members &c

1st Took into Consideration the Conduct of the East Tennessee Baptist Association or there prodedancies Wheather We as a Church Approbate or disapprobate And After A discussion of the same the Church declares that they do disapprobate their procedancies Done by Order of Church.

T. Stephens   C. C.

FIRST SATURDAY IN JUNE 1835

the Church Met and After Worship opened a dore for the Reception of Members &C.

Thomas Stephens   C.C.

FIRST SATURDAY IN JULY 1835

the Church met and After Divine Worship opened a dore for the Reception of Members &c

next the Church Appointed a Comitty to Write a leter of these principles to send to Chestua Meeting house agreeable to the Request of Sweetwater Church And apoint Bruther George Stephens and Solomon Sumsy to bare said leter the Commity Thomas Stephens, George Stephens, Solomon Sumsy, William Higgins & Jacob Paige.

Thos. Stephens   C.C.

ON FRIDAY THE TENTH OF JULY 1835

the Church met and Worship. opened a Dore for the Reception &c

First the Church Appointed Mathew Cunningham Assistant deligate to Chestua Meeting house.

Thomas Stephens   C.C.

FIRST SATURDAY IN AUGUST 1835.

The Church met and after Worship opened a dore for the reception of Members

　　　1st　the Church Received the procedances of the Association
helt at Chestua Chirch on the 26th of July 1835　then Appointed George
Stephens　Solomon Sumey and Mathew Cunningham as Deligates to the Association And Appointed Brother Thomas Stephens to Write A letter to the
Association then the Church purtishion Mt. Pleasant, Sweetwater, Rockhill
and New Providence for their Miniterial helps.

Thos. Stephens　C.C.

FRIDY BEFORE THE FIRST SATURDAY IN SEPT. A. D. 1835.

　　　Church Met And after Worship opened her dors for the Reception
of members　then adjourned until Saturday.

　　　Met Agreeable to Adjournment　opened her ders for the Reception
of Members　then Sister Reaney Larrymore applied for a leter of dismission And it Was granted

P-16　　　Church Met a Monday　opened a dore for the Reception of members.

Thomas Stephens　C.C.

FIRST SATURDAY IN OCTOBER 1835

　　　the Church met and After Worship opened a dore for the Reception
of Members.

FIRST SATURDAY IN NOVEMBER 1835

　　　the Church met and after Worship opened a dore for the Reception
of Members　Received Kinney Renfrow by Recantation

FIRST SATURDAY IN DECEMBER 1835.

　　　Church Met and After Worship opened a dore for the Reception of
members &c

FIRST SATURDAY IN JANUARY 1836

　　　Church met and after Worship opened a dore for the Reception
of members &c.

FIRST SATURDAY IN FEBRUARY 1836

the Church met And after Worship opened a dore for the reception
of members and received Elizabeth Rose by leter &c

Thomas Stephens   C.C.

FIRST SATURDAY IN MARCH 1836

Church met and After Worship opened a dore for the Reception
of Members &c

FIRST SATURDAY IN APRILE 1836

Church met and after Worship Opened a dore for the reception
of members &c.

FIRST SATURDAY IN MAY 1836

Church met and After Worship Opened a dore for the reception of
members &c

FIRST SATURDAY IN JUNE 1836

Church met and after Worship opened a dore for the Reception
of Members &c then Brother Solomon Sumey and Wife Ruthy Sumey also
Brother William Higgans and Wife Polly Higgans aplied for leters of dismishion And the Church granted them All leters. Sign by order of the
Church

Thos. Stephens   C.C.

FIRST SATURDAY IN JULY 1836

the Church met and after Worship opened a dore for the Reception
of Members &c -

FIRST SATURDAY IN AUGUST 1836

Church met And after Worship opened a dore for the Reception of
members &c.

1st Appointed Brother Clark to Write a leter to the Association
Also Apointed Brother George Stephens and Jerrymiah Cunningham to bare said
leter as Delligates to the Association then Appointed a Communion Meeting

to Commence Friday before the first Saturday in Sept next and agreed to pertishion hur sisters Churches for helps to atend us to Wit Mt. Pleasant, Pleasant Grove, and Mt. Zion, and Apointed   (P-17)   Brother Preston J. B. Melton an John Carter to bare said pertishions

Sign by Order of the Church.

Thos Stephens, C. C.

FRIDAY BEFORE THE FIRST SATURDAY IN SEPT. 1836.

Church Met and After Worship opened a dore for the Reception of members And received by leter John and Matilda Mashburn And Dismissed by Leter Ellender Blaids and adjorned until Saturday.

Met acordan to Apointment opned a dore for the Reception of members And Received by Leter John Cunningham And his Wife Sarah Cunningham Also Sarah Rose by Leter.

Thomas Stephens, C. C.

FIRST SATURDAY IN OCTOBER 1836

Church met And After Worship Opened a dore for the Reception of members &c

FIRST SATURDAY IN NOVEMBER 1836

Church met And After Worship opened a dore for the Reception of members &c And Dismissed Sister Nancy Clark by Leter

Thos. Stephens, C. C.

FIRST SATURDAY IN DECEMBER 1836

Church met And after Worship opened a Dore for the Reception of Members, first Our Brother Jasan Matlock rezined unto the Church his pastorial office.

Thos Stephens, C. C.

FIRST SATURDAY IN FEBRUARY 1837

Church met And After Worship opened a dore for the Receptions of members And Received by Letter Zaciariah Rose and purtishioned Mt. Pleasant Church Brothers to Attend as our pastor Also Changing our meeting from the first to the Third.

Thos. Stephens, C. C.

3RD SATURDAY IN APRILE 1837

Church met And after Worship opened A dore for the Reception of Members and Received Elisha Laws And his Wife Ellender Laws by Letter, then the Church brought in a Charge Against Brother George Christian for Disorderly Conduct and Apointed Brother Z. Rose and G. Stephens to Cite him to the next meeting in Course, then Sister Susannah West aplide for a letter of Dismishion and it was granted then the Church adjorned until Sabbath then opened a dore for the Reception of members And received the following persons by Letters to Wit James Laws, Nancy Laws, Elizabeth Angeline Laws, Fanny Laws, Dinah Laws, & Elisha Laws.

Signed by order of the Church

Thos. Stephens, C.C.

P-18   THIRD SATURDAY IN MAY 1837

Church met and after Worship opened a dore for the Reception of members

1st Chose Brother Alferd King to the pastoral Care of the Church then Recd Manurvy Hicks by Letter, also Recvd Margaret Harden by Experience then took up the Refferance from Last meeting to this Against Brother George Christian And After hearing him declared an unfellowship with him.

THIRD SATURDAY IN JUNE 1837

Church met and After Worship opened a dore for the Reception of Members.

1st Apointed Brother Z. Rose, Clark pro tem

2ndly Owing to some difficulty the Church refered the Baptism of Mass Harden to next meeting

3rdly the Church Agreed to have a sacrimental Season in July the Church agreed to purtishion New Providence, Pleasant Grove, Zion Hill for there helps to Attend us.

Z. Rose, Clerk pro tem

FRIDAY BEFORE THE 3RD SATURDAY IN JULY 1837

Church met and after Worship opened a dore for the Reception of Members

Church met And after Worship opened a dore for the Reception of members

1st the Church took up the Refferance from last Meeting to this concerning Mrs. Harden, and Agreed to baptise her then Adjorned until Saturday

Thos. Stephens, C. C.

Met acordan to adjournment opened a dore for the Reception of Members and Received Margaret Leonard by Letter

3RD SATURDAY IN AUGUST 1837

Church met and After Worship opened a dore for the Reception of Members and received Lewis M. Howel and his Wife Sarah Howel And dismissed by letter Wm Ray

Signed by order of the Church the day above written

Thos Stephens, C. C.

THIRD SATURDAY IN SEPT 1837

Church met And proceeded to business

1st Chose Brother D. A. Walker, Clerk pro tem for the day

2ndly Sister Elizabeth Rose aplide for letters of Dismishion and it Was granted.

Thos. Stephens, C. C.

NOVEMBER 3RD SATURDAY 1837

Church met And After Worship proceeded to business

1st Apointed Brother Joab Hill Moderator protem

2ndly Apointed Z. Rose Clark protem

3rdly the Church took up the Request of Brother G. Stephens
P-19 to Apoint Another Deacon And After some Consideration the Church Agreed to defer it untill next meeting.

Z. Rose, Clark protem

DECEMBER 3rd SATURDAY 1837

Church Met And after Divine Worship Proceded to Business

1st took up the Refferance of last meeting to this and after some discussion it was Agreed to lay it over until the Church Call for it

2ndly Brother Mathew Cunningham Applied for a letter of dismission and the Church granted him one.

Thos Stephens, C. C.

2ND SATURDAY IN FEBRUARY 1838

Church met And afterWorship proceeded to Business

1st Appointed Brother Z. Rose Clark protem

2ndly Caled for the Records of the Church on the subject of procuring a Minister to atent hur and to take the Ceare of the Church Result —Elder John Givens Chose unanimously by the Church

3rdly Appointed Brother G. Stephens & Z. Rose to bare a purtishion to Mount Zion to there next meeting (it being the plase Where Brother Givens has his membership) for the purpose of obtaining that Church's Consent.

Z. Rose, Clerk protem

2ND SATURDAY IN FEBRUARY 1838

Church met and after Worship Chose Brother Joab Hill Md. protem then opened a dore for the reception of members.

Thos Stephens, C. C.

2ND SATURDAY IN MARCH 1838

Church Met and After Worship opened a dore for the reception of members And received Solomon Horton and his Wife Nancy by letter Then Dismissed Jacob Page by Letter. Then the Church agreed to alter hur meeting days from the 3rd to the 1st Saturday then Adjourned untill Evning

Met pursned to adjournedment then the Church brought a Charge Against Brother James, a Collered Brother for the profain Language and after some Discushion of the same it was Agreed to lay it over untill next meeting and Appointed Brother Solomon Horton and Willis A. Collerred

Brother to Site him to the next meeting.

Thos. Stephens, C. C.

APRILE 1ST SATURDAY 1838

Church Met And After Worship proceeded to Business

1st Apointed Z. Rose Clark protem

2ndly took up the Charge Against Brother James, a Collerred man and After (P-20) hearing him excumacated him from fellowship As A Disorderly member Done in Church Conferance

Z. Rose, Clerk protem

JUNE 1ST SATURDAY 1838

Church met And After Worship opened a door for the Reception of members and Received John H. Laws By Experience

2ndly Agreed to purtishion Mt. Pleasant, Pleasant Grove and New Providence for their ade at our August Meeting.

Thos. Stephens, C. C.

JULY, 1ST SATURDAY, 1838

Church Met And proceeded to business

1st Apointed Brother A. D. Walker Clark protem for the day, then Opened a dore for the reception of Members And received J. Jarvis And Polly Jarvis, his Wife By letters.

D. A. Walker, C. pro

FRIDAY BEFORE THE FIRST SATURDAY IN SEPTEMBER 1833.

Church Met And After Worship opened a dore for the reception of members

1st Choise Brother Soloman Horton to the office of a Deacon iff found orthodox in faith

2ndly Ordered the Clark to Write A letter to the Association And have it at next meeting for inspection, then Apointed Brother Zacariah

Rose Dawson A Walker to bare said letter to the association.

3rdly Agreed to send up to the Association $1.50 to defray expence of the Association, fifty Cts of said Association and next to our Minutes the brother Jeremiah Cunningham And his Wife Amy Cunningham Aplide for Letters of Dismission And it Was granted then adjorned until Saturday 11 O'Clock. Met pursuant to Adjournedment After Divine Worship opened a dore for the Reception of members And Received Elizabeth Stephens by Letter Isabellah Stephens by Experience then Agreed to Join to the Ordination of Brother Solomon Horton at Oct. Meeting As a Deacon Iff found Orthodox in faith

P-21 Then Agreed to Purtishion Mt Pleasant, Pleasant Grove, Mt. Zion & New Providence Churches for there aide to Attend us on the 1st Saturday in Oct. next in Order to join the Ordination of S. Horton then Adjorned until Sabbath morning 10 O'Clock. Met After Divine Worship Adjorned untill Evning. Met and After Divine Worship opened A dore for the reception of members and received Adline Hardin By experience then adjourned untill Monday 10 O'Clock Met Andafter Divine Worship Came to a Close.

Thos. Stephens, C. C.

FIRST SATURDAY IN AUGUST 1838

Church Met and After Divine Worship opened a dore for the Reception of members

1st Apointed Brother Dawson A Walker Clark protem for the day,

2ndly Granted Brother Zacariah Rose the Liberty of Exercising his Gift at home or Any of hur sister Churches When Caled on so to do, then Adjorned untill Sabbath

Met acordan to adjornedment And after Divine Worship opened a dore for the Reception of members. Then the Association Letter Caled for read and received then the Church gaive our Brothers Delligates to the Association Liberty to Contribute something more to Defray the expence of the Association iff neaded,

D. A. Walker, C. P.

1ST SATURDAY IN OCT. 1838

Church Met And After Worship opened A dore for the Reception of Members

1st James Laws prais the Church to Reconsider his caise upon his exclusion And After some Discushion of the saim the Church grants him a new hearing And laid it over Untill next Meeting, And Apointed Breathern Z. Rose J. Hitower, J. Cunningham and S. Horton to set as a Comity to hear Evidence for And Against James Laws And Report to next meeting.

Then the Church brought in a Charge Against Brother Absolom Prestwood for profain langueague and Apointed Brother Thomas Stephens and Solomon Horton to talk to him Between this and next meeting.

P-22   the Church Allso Apointed Brother John Cunningham And John Hitower to invite Brother Thos. Renfrow to his meeting, then Adjorned.

Met A Sabbathafter Worship opened a dore for the Reception of Members And received A Collered man by experience named Perry Belonging to friend Lowery then Adjorned

Met at Candle lite After Worship opened a dore for the Reception of members And received a Collered Woman by experience named Milly Belonging to friend Harmon then Adjorned.

Thomas Stephens, C. C.

1ST SATURDAY IN NOVEMBER 1838

Church Met And After Divine Worship opened A Dore for the Reception of members And received Rachel Harmon by Experience. Then took up the Case of James Laws And after hearing All the evidence for and Against him restores him to fellowship.

Then took up the Charge Against Brother Absolom Prestwood and After hearing from him Declars unfellowship Against him.

then the Church brought in A Charge Against Brother Thos Renfrow for gambling and disobeying the order of the Church by refusing to Atend meeting And After hearing from him declares unfellowship With him.

Then Sisters Elander Melton, Elizabeth Clark aplide for letters of dismission which was granted

Then received a Letter from Fork Creek requesting of us to alter our Church Meeting days from the 1st Saturday in the month to the 2nd Saturday Which Was Agreed to After December

D. A. Walker, Clark protem

1ST SATURDAY IN DECEMBER 1838

Church Met And After Divine Worship opened a Dore for the Reception of members &c.

Thos. Stephens   C. C.

2ND SATURDAY IN JANUARY 1839

Church Met And After Divine Worship opened a dore for the Reception of members &c

P-23   1st   Sister Rachael Willmouth Aplied for a Letter of dismission Which Was granted.

                                        Thomas Stephens   C. C.

2ND SATURDAY IN FEBRUARY 1839

Church Met And after Worship opened a dore for the Reception of Members &c.

1st   Sister Levina Horton And Sister Mary Join Harrell Aplied for Letters of dismission Which Was granted

                                        Thomas Stephens   C. C.

2ND SATURDAY IN MRCH 1839

the Church Met And After Divine Worship opened a dore for the Reception of Members

1st   Brother Z. Rose aplied for himself and Wife A letter of dismission Which Was granted

2ndly the Church took up a Charge Against Sister Aidline Hardin for lying With a young man And saying thay was Married when thay was not Married for Which the Church declars an unfellowship Against her.

3rdly Brother Bartlet Renfrow Aplied for A letter of Dismishion for himself And Wife Winney Which Was Granted.

                                        James Jarvis
                                        Clark protem

APRILE 2nd SATURDAY 1839

Church Met And After Worship opened a dore for the Reception of Members &c.

                                        T. Stephens, C. C.

MAY 2ND SATURDAY 1839

Church Met and After Worship opened a dore for the reception
of Members &c.

Thos. Stephens C. C.

Caroline Walker diede

JUNE 2nd SATURDAY 1839

Church Met And After Worship opened a dore for the Reception
of Members &c

Nancy Harrell Died.

P-24   JULY 2ND SATURDAY 1839

Church Met And After Worship opened A dore for the Reception
of members And Received John Hitower and his Wife Mary by Letter And
Jain Branston By Experience. Then Apointed our Sacremential Season to
Come on in October And Agreed to purtishion Union, McMinn, Mt. Pleasant,
Pleasant Grove, Big Creek and New Providence Churches for there aide at
Oct. meeting, Cairers to bear said purtishions to Wit Breathern George
Stephens to McMinn, James Jarvis to Mt. Pleasant Lewis Howell to Pleas-
ant Grove, Elder Givens to Big Creek. Delligates to the Associations to
New Providence then Agreed to put in the hands of their Delligates to
the Association $1.25 to defray the expence of the Association.

Then Apointed their Clark to Write A letter to send to the Association And bring it farred to next meeting for inspection And Appointed Brother John Cunningham and Brother James Jarvis to bare said Letter
to the Association.

Thos. Stephens, Church Clark

AUGUST 2ND SATURDAY 1839.

Church Met and After Divine Worship Opened a Dore for the Reception of Members &c then Caled for the Assotiation letter red and received.

Thos Stephens   C. C.

SEPT. 1839

No meeting.

FRIDAY BEFORE THE 2ND SATURDAY IN OCTOBER 1839

Church Met And After Divine Worship opened A dore for the Reception of Members &c

1st Agreed to go into the Example of feet washing on Saturday night Then Adjorned untill Saturday 11 o'Clock

Met pursuant to Adjournment After Worship opened a dore for the Reception of Members &c.

Thos Stephens, C. C.

P-25   NOVEMBER 2ND SATURDAY 1839

Churoh met And After Divine Worship opened a dore for the Reception of Members &c.

Thos. Stephens, C. C.

DECEMBER -

No meeting

JANUARY 2ND SATURDAY 1840

Church Met And After prayer proceded to business

1st Apointed Brother John Mashburn Clark protem

2nd Opened a dore for the reception of members &c

John Mashburn
Clark protem

P-26   FEBRUARY 2ND SATURDAY 1840

Church Met and After preaching proceeded to Business

1st Brother John Carter returned his letter of Dismission that he obtained from this Church

2ndly took up the Request of Brother Wm Wallis from Big Springs Church praying this Church to notice the Conduct of Brother James Laws in two Cases viz. One for bringing suit against him in three Cases without Cause and not acorden to the Gospel the other one for Sabbath breaking by gearing up his team and Moving a famaly on the Sabbath day with his Waggon And after some Consideration of the same the Church Agreed to Bring in the Above named Cases as Charges Against him and Apointed Breathern Thomas Stephens and Solomon Horton to site Brother James Laws to his next meeting in Corse.

Thos. Stephens C. C.

MARCH SECOND SATURDAY A. D. 1840

Church Met And after preaching proceded to Business

1st Opened a dore for the Reception of members &c

2ndly took up the Referrence Against Brother James Laws from last Meeting to this And After some discussion of the same the Church Layed it over untill next Meeting in Corse.

Thos. Stephens
Church Clark

2ND SATURDAY APRILE 1840

Church Met and After preaching opened a dore for the reception of Members

2ndly took up the referrence Against James Laws from last meeting to this And After hearing him the Church Declars an unfellowship Against him

3rdly Agreed to have A sacremental Season beginning friday before the second Saturday in August next and Agreed to purtishion Pleasant Grove, New Providence, Mt. Zion, Tellico River, Union, McMinn and fore Mile Churches for there ____ Ministerial helps and Apointed Breathern John Carter, Thomas Stephens, Solomon Horton, George Stephens and Elder Givins to bare said purtishions

Signed by order of the Church the day and date above written.

Thomas Stephens C.C.

P-27   MAY 2ND SATURDAY 1840

Church Met and After preaching proceded to Business

1st Apointed Brother Solomon Horton Clark protem for the day

2ndly Opened A Dore for the Reception of members

3rdly Agreed to purtishion Ocoee Church for there Ministerial helps to attend us in August Meeting   then Adjorned untill Sabbath morning   Opened a Dore for the Reception of members andreceived Susannah Fisher by Experience.

Solomon Horton, C. Protem

JUNE 2ND SATURDAY 1840

Church met And After preaching proceded to Business

1st   Opened A dore for the Reception of members and received Malinda Laws By letter and Mary Howard Walker by Experience

2ndly Received the Rules of Decorum Which may be found on the first leaf of this book

Thomas Stephens, C. C.
John Givens, Moderator

JULY 2ND SATURDAY 1840.

Church Met And After prayer opened A Dore for the Reception of members &c.

1st Ordered the Clark to have a letter written to send to the Association and have it at next meeting for inspection

2nd Appointed Breathern George Stephens and Solomon Horton as Delligates to bare said letter to the Association Also Agreed to Donate $1 to Defray the Expence of the Association.

Thomas Stephens, C. C.

FRIDAY BEFORE THE SECOND SATURDAY IN AUGUST 1840

Church met And After Worship opened a dore for the reception of Members then Caled for the Association Letter red And received the Changing the meeting day from the 2nd to the 3rd Saturday

Thos. Stephens

3RD SATURDAY IN SEPT. 1840

Church Met And After preaching opened a Dore for the Reception of Members And Received Larkin Laws by Experience then Adjorned until Evening.

OCTOBER

No meeting.

P-28   3RD SATURDAY IN NOVEMBER 1840

Church met and After preaching opened a dore for reception of members &c.

                                        Thos. Stephens   C. C.

                3RD SATURDAY IN DECEMBER 1840

Church met And After preaching opened a dore for the Reception of members   then Adjorned

Met acordon to Adjournment opened A dore for the Reception the Brother James Laws aplied for Letters of Dismishion for himself and Wife Which Was granted.

                JANUARY 3RD SATURDAY 1841

Church met And After preaching proceded to business

1st Opening a dore for the Reception of members

                3RD SATURDAY FEBRUARY 1841

No Business

                MARCH 3RD SATURDAY 1841

Church Met opened a dore for the Reception of members &c. Sister Sally Harrell aplied for a letter of Dismishion which Was granted.

                        Solomon Horton –

                APRILE 3RD SATURDAY 1841

Church met And After preaching proceed to Business

1st opened a Dore for the Reception of Members

2ndly Agreed to purtishion Ocoee Church for there Ministerial helps to attend us the Friday before the third Saturday in August next.

Thos. Stephens   C.C.

MAY 3RD SATURDAY 1841

Church Met And after preaching proceeded to Business

1st Apointed brother Lee, Moderator for the day

2ndly Opened a dore for the Reception of Members &c.

Thos. Stephens, C. C.

JUNE 3RD SATURDAY 1841

Church Met And after preaching proceded to Business

1st Opened a dore for the Reception of members

2ndly Agreed to purtishion the following (P-29) Churches for there Ministerial helps to Attend us on Friday before the 3rd Saturday in August next viz Four Mile, Connesaggy, Pleasant Grove, New Providence, Union, McMinn and Apointed the following Breathern to bare said purtishion to Wit James Jarvis, Thos Stephens

3rdly Sister Elizabeth Walker aplied for a Letter of Dismisshion Which was granted.

Thos. Stephens, C. C.

JULY

No Meeting.

FRIDAY BEFORE THE 3RD SATURDAY IN AUGUST 1841

Church Met And After preaching proceded to Business

1st Opening a dore for the Reception of members &c.

2nd Ordered the Clark to Write a letter to the Association and have it at next meeting for inspection and apointed Breathern John Mashburn And George Stephens to bare said letter to them.

3rdly the Church brought a Charge Against Sister Elizabeth Adaline Laws for a sin of fornication an Declared an Unfellowship Against her for said sin.

Thomas Stephens, C.C.

THIRD SATURDAY IN SEPT. 1841

Church Met and After preaching proceded to business

1st Opened A dore for the Reception of Members.

Katharine Harrill, deceased

Thos. Stephens, Clark

3RD SATURDAY IN OCT. 1841

Church Met & After preaching proceded to Business

1st Opened a Dore for the Reception of Members

2ndly Brother Andrew McNabb & Sally McNabb aplied for Letters of Dismission, Which Was granted.

Thos. Stephens, C. C.

3RD SATURDAY IN NOVEMBER 1841

Church Met And After Worship opened a Dore for the Reception of Members & Received Marry Jain Harrill by Letter

Solomon Horton, protem Church Clark

P-30   3RD SATURDAY IN JANUARY 1842

Church met and After preaching proceed to Business

1st Apointed Elder C. Sanders Moderator for the day

2ndly Opened a Dore for the Reception of Members

3rdly Received a Purtishion from Fork Creek Church praying us to send them some of our Members to set with them at February Meeting in Order to Consider the propriety or impropriety of the Dissolution of the Church. We therefore Agree to send Thos Stephens, George Stephens, Solomon Horton & John Cunningham to set with them.

4th Sister Fanney Laws aplied for Letters or Dismishion for Elisha Laws & Ellenner Laws which was granted

Thos Stephens, C. C.

3RD SATURDAY IN FEBRUARY 1842

Church Met And After Worship opening a Dore for the Reception of Members and Received George Long & Elijah Laws by Letter

3RD SATURDAY IN APRILE 1842

Church mt And After preaching opened a Dore for the Reception of Members

2ndly Sister Mary Prestwood aplied for a letter of Dismishion Which Was Granted.

Thomas Stephens, Clark

1842 JUNE 3 SATURDAY

P-31   1842 July 3 Saturday. Church Met And after preaching opened a dore for the Reception of Members &c.

2ndly Agreed to purtishion the following Churches for the Ministeral & Deacon And to Attend us on Friday before the 3rd Saturday in Oct. 1842 that is to say Union, McMinn, Pleasant Grove, New Providence & Bethlehem

3rdly Ordered the Clark to Write a letter to send to the Association And have it At Sept Meeting for inspection And Apointed Breathern Thos. Stephens And Solomon Horton to bare the same letter

4thly Agreed to purtishion for the next Association and also to resind and act upon at the Association in 1837, Article 13th.

1842, August 3 Saturday.

1st Church Met And after preaching opened a dore for the Reception of members And received Lenzy Nicholson by Experience

2ndly the Church brought a Charge Against Brother Larkin W. Laws for lying and after some discushing of the same layed it over until next Meeting in Corse & Agreed to bear Affidavids as would against him.

Solomon Horton
Clark protem

SEPT 3 SATURDAY 1842

1st Church Met And After preaching opened a dore for the reception of members &c.

2ndly took up the Refference Against Brother Larkin W. Laws and after some discushion of the same the Church Agreed to lay it over untill Friday before the 2nd Saturday in Oct. 1842

Church met And acordan to Adjornedment proceded to business

1st Opened a dore for the reception of members

2ndly took up the Charge Against Brother Larkin W. Laws and for said Crime Excluded him from the fellowship of the Church, then adjorned

Thomas Stephens, Clark

P-32   FRIDAY BEFORE THE 3RD SATURDAY IN OCT. 1842

Church met And After preaching opened a dore for the Reception of Members

2ndly Adjorned until Saturday

Met opened a dore for the Reception of members then Sister Zilpha Christian Aplide for A Letter of Dismishion Which was granted, then Received Triplet by Recantation.

3RD SATURDAY IN NOV. 1842

Church Met and proceded to business

1st Opened a Dore for the Reception of members & Received Sally Jain Walker and Nancy Walker by Experience

2ndly Sister Mary H. Browder, Fanny Laws, Dinah Laws, Elizabeth Laws and Brother Elijah Laws aplied for Letters of Dismishion Which Was granted

3rdly the Church Took a Charge Against Brother Lewis M. Howell for sensoring the Church and then Agreed to Lay it over until next meeting in Corse then Adjorned.

Thos. Stephens, C. C.

3RD SATURDAY IN DECEMBER 1842

Church Met and proceded to Business

1st Opened a Dore for the Reception of Members And received Benjamin R. Sands by Experience And Abraham Hann and his Wife named Jain by Letter

2ndly took up the Refferance Against Brother Lewis M. Howell and Excluded him from the fellowship of the Church

3rdly Took up a Charge against Sister Tally Howell for Disorderly (or) vicious Conduct towards the Church and for said crime Excludes hur from the fellowship of the Church

4thly Apointed Brother Thos Stephens and James Jarvis to invite Brother Preston, G. B. Melton to Atend our next Meeting in corse then adjorned.

Thos. Stephens, Church Clark

P-33   3RD SATURDAY IN JANUARY 1843

Church met and after preaching opened a dore for the reception of members &c Then Brother Dawson A Walker Aplied for a letter of Dismishion Which Was Granted.

Thos. Stephens, C. C.

3RD SATURDAY IN FEBRUARY 1843

Church met And After preaching opened a Dore for the Reception of Members &c

Thos. Stephens, C. C.

3RD SATURDAY IN MARCH 1843

Church met And after preaching opened a Dore for the reception of members &c.

1st Apointed Brother Jas. Jarvis Clark for the day

2nd the Church took a Charge Against Brother Preston G. B. Melton for Disobeying the Church And Apointed Brother Thos Stephens and James Jarvis to Cite him to hur next meeting in Corse

signed by order of the Church the day above written

Jas Jarvis
Clark protem

3RD SATURDAY IN APRILE 1843

3RD SATURDAY IN APRILE 1843

The Church Met andafter preaching proceded to Business

1st Opened a Dore for the Reception of Members &c

2ndly took up the refference Against Brother P. G. B. Melton and Agrees to Lay it over untill Called for then Adjourned

signed by order of the Church the day And Date above Written.

Thos. Stephens, Clark

3RD SATURDAY IN JUNE 1843

Church Met and After preaching proceeded to Business

1st Opened a Dore for the Reception of members

2ndly Sister Susan Fisher Aplied for a Letter of Dismishion which Was granted

3rdly took up the request of Last Year's Association wheather or not we will take up a Corresponance with the Tennessee Association under the title of the Primitive Baptist Association or not. We Answer we will not take up a Corresponance with them under that name

4thly Granted Brother Willis the liberty of Exercising his gift in the bonds of his Church

Signed by order of the Church

Thos. Stephens, C. Clark

3RD SATURDAY IN JULY 1843

Church Met And After preaching proceded to Business

1st Opened a Dore for the Reception of members &c.

2ndly the Church took up a Charge Against Brother Perry a man of coller for joining the Convention baptist and for said Crime Declared an unfellowship against him.

Thos Stephens, C.C.

3RD SATURDAY IN AUGUST 1843

Church met and after preaching proceded to business

1st opened a dore for the Reception of members

2ndly took up the Refferance Against Brother P. G. B. Melton for disobeying the Church And after some Deliberation on the same Declared an unfellowship Against him

3rd Ordered the Clark to Write A Letter to send up to the Association and Apointed Brother Thos Stephens, Benjamin R. Sands to bare the said letter

Thos Stephens, C. Clark

P-35   3RD SATURDAY IN SEPTEMBER 1843

The Church met and after preaching proceded to Business

1st Opened a dore for the reception of members

2nd Galed for the Letter to send up to the Association Red and Received then adjorned untill next meeting in Corse

Thos. Stephens, C. C.

3RD SATURDAY IN OCTOBER 1843

The Church met and after preaching opened a dore for the reception of members

3RD SATURDAY IN NOV. 1843

The Church Met and After preaching opened a dore for the Reception

3RD SATURDAY IN DEC. 1843

the Church met and after preaching opened a dore for the Reception of members

3RD SATURDAY IN JAN. 1844

the Church Met and after preaching opened a dore for the Reception of members & then Apointed Brother Benjamin R. Sands Assistant Clark

Thos. Stephens,
Church Clark

3RD SATURDAY IN FEB. 1844

the Church met and after prayer opened a Dore for the Reception of members &c

P-36   3RD SATURDAY IN MARCH

Church met and after preaching opened a dore for the Reception of members

3RD SATURDAY IN MAY 1844

Church Met and after preaching proceded to business

1st Opened a dore for the Reception of members and Received by letter Joseph, Anna, Matilda, Jain, Charity, and Joseph Davis, Junior and Dismissed by Letter Mary Jane Harrell and Matilda Laws then adjorned

Thos Stephens, C. C.

3RD SATURDAY IN JUNE 1844

Church Met and After preaching proceded to Buisness

1st Opened a dore for the reception of members

2ndly Apointed A Sacremental meeting commencing friday before the 3rd Saturday in Sept. next and agreed to purtishion the following Churches for helps to Attend us on that occasion to Wit, Union, McMinn, New Hopewell, New Friendship, Ocoee, Bethlehem and Spring Town and then adjorned.

Thos. Stephens, C. C.

3RD SATURDAY IN JULY 1844

No meeting

3RD SATURDAY IN AUGUST 1844.

P-37   FRIDAY BEFORE 3RD SATURDAY SEPT. 1844

Church met And after Worship proceded to Buisness

1st Opened a dore for the Reception of members then Adjorned till Saturday opened a dore for the reception of members and Dismissed Sarah Barnett by letter, then Adjorned till Sabbath

Met and adjorned till Evening.

Opening a dore for the reception of members And Received by experience Nancy Worric, Katharine Warric and Nancy Bell, then received the Letter to the Association was received then Adjorned.

Thos Stephens, C. C.

3RD SATURDAY OCT. 1844

Church met and no business done.

3RD SATURDAY IN NOV. 1844

Church met and no business done.

3RD SATURDAY IN DECEMBER 1844

The Church met and after preaching proceded to buisness Next opened a dore for the reception of members and Apointed Brother Jarvis Clark. Dismissed Katharine Warric by Letter and then Adjorned.

Thos Stephens, C. C.

3RD SATURDAY IN JANUARY 1845

Church met and done no buisness

P-38   ### 3RD SATURDAY IN APRILE 1845

Church met And After Warship proceded to buisness

1st Opening A dore for the Reception of members

2ndly Recinded an act granting sister Susan Fisher A Letter of Dismishion

3rdly the Church brought a Charge Against Sister Susan Fisher for an Act of fornication and After hearing the testimony against hur declared an unfellowship with hur   then Adjorned.

Thos. Stephens, C. C.

3RD SATURDAY IN MAY 1845

The Church Met and after preaching proceded to buisness

1st Apointed brother James Jarvis Clark protem for the day

2ndly opened a dore for the Reception and received by letter Thomas Wallis

3RD SATURDAY IN JUNE 1845

the Church met and after preaching proceded to buisness

1st Opened a dore for the Reception of members &c

3RD SATURDAY IN JULY 1845

the Church met & After preaching proceded to buisness

1st Opened a dore for the reception of members

2ndly Agreed to have a Sacremental Meeting Commensing Friday before the 3rd Saturday in October next and agreed to purtishion Mt. Pleasant, Bethlehem, Ocoee and Union, McMinn Churches to Attend us on that occasion

3rdly Ordered the Clark to Wright a letter to send up to the Association and have it red at next meeting and Apointed Breathren George Stephens and Absolom Hawn to bare the same to them.

Thos Stephens, C. C.

P-39   ### 3RD SATURDAY IN AUGUST 1845

the Church met And after preaching proceded to Buisness

1st Opened a dore for the Reception of members &c

Thos Stephens, C. C.

3RD SATURDAY IN SEPTEMBER 1845

Church met and after preaching proceded to Buisness

1st Opened a dore for the reception of members &c

Thos. Stephens, C. C.

FRIDAY BEFORE THE 3RD SATURDAY IN OCTOBER 1845

The Church met And After preaching proceded to buisness

1st Opened a dore for the reception of members then Adjorned untill Saturday

Met pursuant to Adjournment opened a dore for the Reception of members then Adjorned till Sabbath

Met pursuant to adjournment After preaching opened a dore for the Reception of members &c. Adjorned untill Monday

Met pursuant to Adjournment opened a dore for the Reception of members &c and then Met and Adjorned, divrs time through the Weak and induring that time Received by experience Polly Ann Henderson, Seth Walker, George Williams, and Andrew Nicholson and on Monday following Received Nancy Ray by Experience.

Thos. Stephens, Clark

P-40   3RD SATURDAY IN NOVEMBER 1845

the Church met and after preaching opened a dore for the Reception of members and received by Experience James Powers and George Renfrow then adjorned.

Thos. Stephens,
Church Clark

3RD SATURDAY IN DECEMBER 1845

the Church met and After preaching proceded to Buisness

1st Opened for the Reception of members

2ndly Released Brother George Stephens from being Treasurery for the Church and Apointed Brother Jos James (senior) in his stid.

Thos Stephens, Clark

3RD SATURDAY IN JANUARY 1846

the Church met and after preaching proceded to Buisness

the Church met and after preaching proceded to Buisness

1st Opening a dore for the Reception of Members &c

Thos. Stephens, C. C.

3RD SATURDAY IN MARCH 1846

the Church met and after preaching proceded to Buisness

1st Apointed Brother Solomon Horton Clark protem for the day

2ndly the Church brought a Charge Against Sister Judy Ray for giving bad advice to young members by saying it is no harm to dance nor play the fiddle.

3rdly the Church Apointed Brother Jas Sands his Wife and Sister Sarah Cunningham to Cite hur to the next meeting.

Solomon Horton, C. protem

P-41   ### 3RD SATURDAY IN APRILE 1846

the Church met & After preaching proceded to buisness

1st Opened a dore for the reception of members

2ndly Caled for the Referance of Last meeting to this Whare apon (Whereupon) Sister Judy Ray Came farred and stated to the Church that the Charge taken against hur is fals whar a pon the Church Layed it over Untill next Meeting in Order to have the evidence of Brother James Powers in as much as the Charge was brought by the testimony of him and the said Powers being Absance the Church Apointed Brother John Hitower & George Long to notify him that the Church request of him to Attend hur next meeting.

Thos Stephens, C. Clark

3RD SATURDAY IN MAY 1846

the Church Met and after preaching 1st Opening A dore for the Reception of members And received Sister Unice Fare, Wm C. Lee (An ordained Minister) and his Wife Manervy Lee by Letter

2ndly the Church Caled for the Referance againstSister Ray and after some discushion of the saim And the Church postponed it till next Meeting in order to have the Evidence of Sister Polly Ann Cunningham & Apointed Brother Jas Jarvis & Jas Sands to notify hur of that fact

3rdly Ordered the Treasuary Brother Sands to pay out any moneys now in hand to Wm Watson or Thos. Hudson the Church being in debt to them

Thos. Stephens, C. Clark

P-42   3RD SATURDAY IN JUEN 1846

Church Met After preaching proceded to Buisness

1st   Chois Wm C. Lee Clerk protem for the day

2ndly   Took up the Reference against Sister Judy Ray and after the testamony the Church excommunicates her from the fellowship of the Church

3rd   Apointed A sacremental Meeting Commencing Friday before the 3rd Saturday in August next And Agreed to petition Bethlehem Springtown Ocoee & New Hopewell Churches for there Aid to attend on that occasion

4th   Received A petition from Short Creek Church Requesting of us to send them our Minister on the Friday before the 2nd Saturday in July next to Assist in the Ordation of a Minister And to Administer the Lord's Supper Which petition Was Granted.

Wm C. Lee, As. Clerk

3RD SATURDAY IN JULY 1846

The Church MetAnd After preaching proceded to Business

1st   Apointed Brother Wm C. Lee Moderator for the day

2nd   opened a dore for the reception of members

3rd   Received A petition from Mt. Pleasant Church requesting of us to Chainge our meeting day Which petition was received for Consideration.

Thos Stephens, C. Clerk

3RD FRIDAY BEFORE SATURDAY IN AUGUST 1846.

the Church Met And After preaching proceded to Buisness

1st   Apointed Brother Wm C. Lee, Clerk for the day

2ndly   Opened A dore for the Reception of members

3rdly   Ordered the Clerk to Write A Letter to the association

and have it at next meeting for inspection and that   (P-43)   Brother Wm
C. Lee and Abraham Haun bare the saim letters and that the Church send up
one Dollar to defray the Expence of the Association

4th the Church agrees to ask Consel of the Association of And
Concerning receiving Members of Other Baptist Churches on there Baptism
known by Mishionary Baptist Na or May.

5th Received A petition from our sister Church Bethlehem requesting our Minister and Deacons Aid to Assist at Sacremental meeting Commencing friday before the 2nd Saturday in Sept. Which Was Granted.

Wm C. Lee Ac Clerk

3RD SATURDAY IN SEPT. 1846

the Church met and apointed Brother Jas Sands (senior) Moderator
protem then received the letter to send to the Association Then Sister
Nancy Bell & Brother James Powers aplied for letters of dismishion Which
Was Granted then adjorned

Met Sabbath opened a dore for Reception of members the Church
took a charge against Brother Leander Prestwood for secretely putting away
an infant belonging to Nancy Ray & for said Act excludes him from the fellowship of the Church

Thos Stephens, C. Clerk

P-44   3RD SATURDAY IN OCT. 1846

the Church met and after preaching proceded to buisness

1st Opened A dore for the reception of members Apointed Brother
Wm C. Lee Moderator for the day and Brother Jas. Jarvis Clerk for the day

3rdly Brother B. R. Sands & Sister Unica Fare aplied for letters
of Dismishion Which Was granted

4thly The Church Agreed owing to some difference of & opinion
in Respects of Church Government to Renew their Covenant to look After &
to Act in acordance to the Constitution of the Church & to be reconciled
to each other.

5th Apointed A Sacremental meeting Commencing Friday before the
3rd Saturday in Nov. next & Agreed to purtishion the following Churches for
their Aid to attend us in Nov. next to Wit New Hopewell Springtown & Ocoee
& Apointed the following Breathern to bare said purtishion to Wit. Thos.
Wallis, John Hitewer, Jas Jarvis, John Triplet

Jas Jarvis, C. Pretem

FRIDAY BEFORE THE 3RD SATURDAY IN NOV. 1846

the Church Met And after preaching opened a dore for the reception of Members & the Church having gained some information of the Covenant of Brother James Powers (to Wit fiddling & Dancing) The Church received the Act of Sept Meeting of Dismishion him by letter and take a Charge Against him for the above named Conduct and exclude him from the fellowship of the Church.

N.B. The Clerk had not give the letter to J. Powers at the time he was dismissed - The Church adjurned till Saturday.

P-45   3RD SATURDAY IN FEBRUARY 1847

Church met And after preaching proceded to buisness

1st Choised Brother Wm C. Lee Ac. Clerk

2ndly Opened a dore for the Reception of members &c

                                Wm C. Lee, Ac. Clerk

3RD SATURDAY IN MARCH 1847

the Church Met And after preaching opened a dore for the Reception of members

2nd the Church Agreed to invite Breathern John Hitower, George Long & George Renfrow to Attend there next Church Meeting & Appointed the following Breathern to give the invitation to Wit, George Stephens, John Mashburn, John Cunningham, Jas. Sands

P-46   3rdly Receive a petition from Bethlehem Church Requesting of this Church for hur Ministerial help to Assist At a Sacremental Meeting Commencing Friday before the 2nd Saturday in May next Which Was granted.

                                Wm C. Lee, A. C. Clerk

3RD SATURDAY IN APRILE 1847

the Church Met and After preaching proceded to Buisness

1st Opened a dore for the Reception of Members

2nd Caled for the Reference of last meeting to this Brother George Renfrow being prasant stated the reason he had not attended Church was not that he had anything Against the Church but the Leadors Which appears to be Against Wm C. Lea being a member of the Church for not inviting the Mishionaries to preach. the Church released Brother Lea took up the Charge Against Brother John Hitower And upon said Charge excludes him from the fellowship of the Church. Brother George Long being preasant gaive the Church no satisfaction the Church agreed to Lay it over till Caled for; Brother John Triplett stated to the Church that he had done Wrong by getting drunk for Which he was sory for And Wish the Church to forgive him. Which she did; Received a purtishion from Christian Freedom Church Requesting our Ministerial Aid to Assist in a sacremental meeting Commencing on Friday before the 3rd Saturday in June next Which was granted P-47

Wm C. Lee   A. C. Clerk

3RD SATURDAY IN MAY 1847.

the Church met and after Worship proceded to Buisness

1st Opened A dore for the Reception of Members &c.

2nd Received A purtishion from New Prospect Church requesting of this Church to send our ministeral & Deacon Aid to Assist in the Or-dination of Brother L. D. Pearson & to Administer the Lords Supper on Sabbath it being the first Saturday in Sept next & Sabbath following Which Was granted.

Thos. Stephens, Church Clerk

P-48   3RD SATURDAY IN AUGUST 1847

the Church Met and After Preaching proceded to buisness

1st Chois Brother Wm C Lee Moderator protem

2nd Opened a dore for the Reception of Members & Received by Letter Katharine Sherman

3rd Ordered the Clerk to Write A Letter to the Association and have it at next meeting for inspection

4th Apointed Brothers Wm C. Lee & Thos Wallis to bare said Let-ter to the Association

5th the Church agreed to ask for the next association & in Case of failing to Get it she ask for A Communion Meeting

6th the Church Agrees to have a protracted Meeting Commencing Friday before the 3rd Saturday in October next And Agreed to purtishion the following Churches for there Aid to Wit - Springtown, Ocoee, New Friend-ship, Goodfield, Shoal Creek & Antioc

7th received & granted A purtishion from Shoal Creek Church praying of us to send our Ministerial & Deacons to Attend them on Friday before the 2nd Saturday in Sept next on a Sacremental ocasion.

Thos. Stephens, Church Clerk

3RD SATURDAY IN SEPT. 1847

Church Met And After preaching proceded to Buisness

1st Opened a dore for the Reception of Members

2ndly Caled for theLetter to send to the Association Which was received by the Church Clerk

Thos. Stephens, Church Clerk

P-49   3RD SATURDAY IN OCT. 1847

Church Met & After preaching proceded to Buisness

1st Opened a Dore for the Reception of Members &c.

2nd Received & granted A purtishion from Christian Freedom requesting of us our Ministerial Aid to Ordain a deacon

3rd Sister Marthy Melton aplied for a Letter of Dismission Which Was Granted

4th on Monday 18th Received by Letter Sister Katharine Warrick

5th At night granted a Letter of Dismission to Jain Prestwood

6th On Wednesday 20 Received by Experience Elizabeth Daniel & Mary his Wife & Lintha Malissa Richards.

Wm C. Lee, A. C. Clerk

2ND SATURDAY IN NOVEMBER 1847

Church Met & after preaching proceded to business

1st Opened a dore for the reCeption of members & received by Experience Samuel Warrick Thomas Renfrow, Elizabeth Nicholsen & Candis Mashburn

2nd Dismissed by Letter Nancy Walker (non-slon)

3rd At night received by Experience Sally Ann Johnstone

17TH NOV. 1847

Church Met and opened a dore for the Reception of Members & Received by Letter Brother Henry Gan an sister Anna Gan, his Wife and received by Experience Elizabeth Cook and Rebeca Romack on the 18th of the saim month Received as By Letter Sister Henry Long.

Wm Lee, Ac. Clerk

P-50   3RD SATURDAY IN DECEMBER 1847

Church met and after preaching proceded to Buisness

1st Opened a Dore for the Reception of Members & Received By Experience Wm Samples

Thos. Stephens, Church Clerk

3RD SATURDAY IN JANUARY 1848

Church met and After preaching proceded to Buisness

1st Opened a dore for the Reception of Members &c

2nd Received And granted a purtishion from members purpoting to be members of the Sweetwater United Baptist Association Wishing to become Constituted as a Church in said Association.

Thos. Stephens, Church Clerk

3RD SATURDAY IN FEBRUARY 1848

Church met and proceded to Buisness

1st Opened a dore for the Reception of members & Received as By Letter Sister Elizabeth Branham

2nd By the Request of Brother John Givens the Church Released him from being pastor of the Church & Caled Brother Wm C. Lee to the Cear of the sam.

3rd Released Brother Wm C. Lee from being Assistant Clerk for the Church and Apointed Brother Solomon Horton in his plais

Signed by order of the Church the day and date above Written.

Thos Stephens, C. Clerk

3RD SATURDAY IN MARCH 1848

Church met and After prayer proceded to Buisness

1st Opened a Dore for the Reception of members and Received as by Letter Thos Branham

2nd Apointed Brother George Stephens and Thos Wallis to invite Brother Samuel Warrick to attend his next meeting.

P51   3rd Apointed Brother Solomon Horton & Joseph Sands to invite Brother George Williams to Attend his next Meeting

Signed by order of the Church the day and date above Written.

Solomon Horton A. C. Clerk

3RD SATURDAY IN APRILE 1848

Church met and proceded to Buisness

1st opened a dore for the Reception of Members

2ndly the Referance from last Meeting to this Caled for Against Breathern Samuel Warrick, George Williams and Seth Walker, the above named Breathern being preasant gaive the Church satisfaction in general.

Thos. Stephens, Church Clerk

3RD SATURDAY IN MAY 1848

the Church met and after preaching proceded to Buisness

1st Opened a Dore for the Reception of members

3rd Saturday in June 1848 The Church Met and after preaching proceded to Buisness

1st Opened a Dore for the Reception of members &c

Thos Stephens, Church Clerk

P-52   3RD SATURDAY IN AUGUST 1848

The Church Met And after Preaching proceded to Buisness

1st Opened a dore for the Reception of members and Received by Experance Mary Ann Lenard and Dismissed by Letter Sister Mary Ann Henderson (now Chrisp)

2nd Ordered the Clerk to have the Association letter Redy by next Meeting for inspection

    3rd Apointed Breathern Wm C. Lee & James Jarvis to bare the sam to the Association

    4th Agreed to send one Dollar to the Association to help bare the Expence of the saim

    5th the Church Apointed Breathren James Jarvis And John Mashburn to invite Brother Samuel Warrick to Attend his next meeting in order to Clear up some reports to Wit Drunkness, Swaring and the attempt of fiting

    6th Agreed to have A Sacremental Meeting Commencing friday before the 3rd Saturday in November next and agreed to petition All the Churches in the Sweetwater Association Which has Ordain Ministers inn And that the Clerk superintend the saim.

                   T. Stephens, Church Clerk

3RD SATURDAY IN SEPT. 1848

Church met And After preaching proceed to Buisness

    1st Apointed Brother James Shelton Mod. for the day

    2nd Apointed Brother Tinzey Nicholson Clerk for the day

    3rd Opened a dore for the Reception of members &

    4th Brother Thos Branham And his Wife Aplied for Letters of Dismission Which Was granted

    5th Called for the Referance Against Brother Samuel Warrack from Last Meeting to this Brother Warrack being presant gaive satisfaction

P-53   6th Received and granted A purtishion from Bethlehem Church Requestion of us to send aid to them on friday before the 2nd Saturday in Oct. next in Order to go into the Ordination of A Minister and help on a sacremental ocasion.

                   Thos. Stephens, C. Clerk

3RD SATURDAY IN OCT. 1848

Church met and After prayer proceded to Buisness

    1st Opened a dore for the Reception

    2nd Brother Tinzy and Andrew And Sister Elizabeth Nicholson aplied for Letters of Dismishion Which was granted.

Thos Stephens, C. Clerk

3RD SATURDAY IN NOVEMBER 1848.

Church met and After preaching proceded to Buisness

1st Opened A dore for the Reception of members &c.

T. Stephens, C. Clerk

3RD SATURDAY IN DECEMBER 1848

Church Met And After preaching proceded to Buisness

1st Opened a dore for the Reception of members

2nd Received and granted A petition from Union, McMinn Church praying us to grant them our minister to Wit Wm C Lee to attend and take Care of their Church as paster Which privilege is granted to Brother Lee.

Thos Stephens, Church Clerk

3RD SATURDAY IN JANUARY 1849

Church met - No buisness done.

T. Stephens, C. C.

3RD SATURDAY IN FEBRUARY 1849

Church met And After preaching proceded to Buisness

1st Opened A dore for the Reception of members

2nd Sister Matilda Sends (now Blakely) Aplied for a Letter of Dismishion Which Was Granted.

Thos. Stephens, C. C.

P-54   ### 3RD SATURDAY IN MARCH 1849

Church met And After preaching proceded to Buisness

1st Opened a dore for the Reception of Members

2nd   the Church took a Charge Against Brother George Williams &
Henry Gan for Drunkness and apointed Brother George Stephens & John Mash-
burn to talk With Brother William & Brother Joseph Cunningham & Elijah Mc-
Daniel to talk or Cite Brother Gan to the Next Meeting in Aprile

Sollmon Horton Ac C.C.

3RD SATURDAY IN MAY 1849

Church met And preaching proceded to Buisness

1st   Apointed Brother John Mashburn Clerk protem for the day

2nd   Opened A door for the Reception of members

3rd Called for the Reference against Brother Henry Gan Brother
Gan not being present it Was Layed over until next meeting And Apointed
Brother G. McDaniel and Samples to site him to this next Meeting

4th   Brother Samuel Warrick Aplied for A Letter of Dismishion
Which Was postpened untill next Meeting.

John Mashburn Ac. Clerk

In the Year 1848 Abraham Hawn & Wm Sands dyed

Thos. Stephens, C. Clerk

P-55   3RD SATURDAY IN JULY 1849

the Church met and after preaching proceded to Buisness

1st   Caled the Church to Order

2nd   Apointed Brother Wm Watson Clerk for the day

3rd   Opened a dore for the Reception of members

4th   Called for the Referance Against Brother Gan Which Was
layed over untill next meeting

5   the Church took a Charge Against Brother Samuel Warrack for
Drunkness and Apointed Brother Elijah McDaniel And George Stephens to notify him of the fact and to attend the next Church Meeting in Corse.

6th   Received and granted a petition from Bethlehem Church requesting of this Church hur Ministerial and Deacon Ade to Assist them in
A sacremental Meeting Commencing friday before the 2nd Saturday in August
next.

Wm Watson, Ac. Clerk

3RD SATURDAY IN AUGUST 1849

Church Met and After preaching proceeded to Buisness

1st Opened a Dore for the Reception of Members

2nd Caled for the Referance Against Brother T. H. Gann for Drunkness and After some Consideration of the same Declared an unfellowship Against him

2nd Caled for the Referance Against Brother Samuel Warrack and owing to the Brothers Apointed to notify him to Attend his meeting it was Layed over untill Next meeting in Corse And Apointed Brother George Williams and Thos Stephens to Notify him to attend next Meeting

3rd Ordered the Clerk to Write A Letter to send to the Association And have it at next meeting for inspection And Apointed Brother Wm C. Lee And Thos Stephens to Bare the same to her And Agreed that the Church send $1 to help Defray the expense of the Association

4th the Church Apointed A Sacramental Meeting Commencing friday before the 3rd Saturday in November next (P-57) and Agreed to petition the following Churches for Ministerial And Deacon Aid to Wit Bethlehem, Goodfield, Rogers Creek, New Prospect & Springtown And Apointed the Delligates to the Association to bare said petitions, then Adjorned

Thos Stephens, C. C.

3RD SATURDAY IN SEPT. 1849

No Meeting

5TH SATURDAY IN SEPT. 1849

Church Met and After preaching proceded to Buisness

1st Dismissed by Letter Brother John Triplet, Sisters Ruthy Fergerson & Mary Ann Cunningham

Thos Stephens, Church Clerk

3RD SATURDAY IN OCT. 1849

No Buisness done —

Thos Stephens,
C. Clerk

FRIDAY BEFORE THE 3RD SATURDAY IN NOVEMBER 1849

the Church met And after preaching proceded to Buisness

1st opened a dore for the Reception of Members And Received by Experience Mary White Sarah Shambee and Sarah Emeline Loyd

2nd Caled for the Referance Against Brother Samuel Warrack Brother Warrick being preasant gave the Church satisfaction 3. Brother George Renfrow Aplied for himself And Wife Letters of Dismishion Which was granted. Brother Samuel Warrack and Sister Jain Haun aplied fir Letters of Dismishion Which was granted

4 the Church brought a charge against Sisters Synthy Cook & Candes Mashburn for an act of fornication and for said Crime Excludes them from the fellowship of the Church

Thos Stephens C. Clerk

P-57   3RD SATURDAY IN APRILE 1850

Church Met and after Preaching proceded to Buisness

1st Opening A dor for the Reception of Members &c Sent a petition to Bethlehem Church for Brother S. Haun to Attend us next meeting.

Thos. Stephens, C. Clerk

3RD SATURDAY IN MAY 1850

Church met and preaching proceded to buisness

1st Choise Brother Samuel Haun Moderator for the day

2nd Opened a dore for the Reception of Members &c

3 Received and granted a petition from Bethlehem Church Requesting us for our Ministerial & Deacon Ade at Sacramental Meeting.

Thos Stephens, Church Clerk

3RD SATURDAY IN JUNE 1850

Church met And After preaching proceded to Buisness

1st Opened a dore for the Reception of members & Received By Letter Sister Susannah Rogan

2 the Church Agreed to have there sacrimental Meeting Annually in Oct.

3 Agreed to purtishion the following Churches for there Ade to attend us the friday Before the 3rd Saturday in Oct. next at there Sacremental Meeting in order to preach the Word and to Administer the Lord's Supper on Sabbath to Wit Bethlehem, Rogers Creek, Good Field N Prospect   (P-58)   And New Friendship and Apointed the following Breathern to bare said petitions to Wit Joseph Sands (senior) George Stephens Wm C. Lee, Joseph Sands, (Jr) and Thos. Stephens then Adjorned

Thos Stephens, C. Clerk

3RD SATURDAY JULY 1850

Church Met And After Preaching proceded to Buisness

1st Opened a dore for the Reception of members

2 Ordered the Clerk to Write a Letter to send to the Association And have it at Sept. Meeting for inspection and Apointed Brethern George Stephens & Wm C Lee to bare the same to them

3 Agreed to send $1. to help Defray the Expence of the Association then adjorned.

Thos. Stephens, C. Clerk

3RD SATURDAY IN AUGUST 1850

No Buisness

Thos Stephens, C. Clerk

3RD SATURDAY IN SEPT. 1850.

Church met And After preaching proceded to Buisness

1st Opened a dore for the Reception of Members

2 Received the Letter to send to the Association

3rd the Church brought a Charge against Brother George Williams for profain Language & for Drunkness and Apointed Breathern Joseph Sands and Thos Stephens to Cite him to hur next meeting and on Friday of said Meeting

4th Sister Rachel Harmon Aplied for a letter of Dismishion which was granted

      5th Received 2 petitions one from New Prospect and the other one from Four Mile Which Was Granted requesting of us to send our Minister

                                    Thos Stephens, C. Clerk

P-59   3RD SATURDAY IN MAY 1851

Christianburg Church met And After preaching Proceded to Buisness

      1st Opened A Dore for the Reception of members

      2nd Received And granted a petition from Four Mile Church Blount County praying us to send our Ministers to their Church for the purpose of Ordaining a Minister & Deacon

      3rd By the information of Brother George Stephens it is Apertained that the Church has in his Hands $4.30 on Motion of Brother Cunningham it is ordered that Brother George Stephens pay himself out of said Money $2.25 Monney paid by him for a peace of land the Church bought of O. L. Walker for a grove

      5th it is ordered that the Balance of the Money Remain in his hands untill Caled for by the Church

                                      Thos. Stephens, C. Clerk

P-60   3RD SATURDAY IN JUNE 1851

      No Meeting on Saturday. Sabbath met After Preach proceded to Buisness

      1st Received & granted A petition from Union, McMinn Church requesting of this Church to send them Ministerial & Deacon ade to attend in August at a sacremental Meeting

      2 Brother Laranzy D. Pearson (Minister of the Gospel) Applied for a Letter of Dismission Which Was Granted

      Signed By order of the Church the day and date above Written

                                  Thos Stephens, Church Clerk

                 3RD SATURDAY IN AUGUST 1851

Church met and prayer proceded to Buisness

1st   Opened a dore for the Reception of Members

2nd   Agreed to petition Springtown, New Friendship and Bethlehem Churches for their Ministerial ade to attend us on Friday before the 3rd Saturday in October next at a Sacremental ocasion and Apointed Breathern Solomon Horton Jos. Sands, George Stephens, James Jarvis, and Wm C. Lee to bare said petitions.

4   Granted Letters of Dismissions to Brother Thos. Renfrow and his Wife, Katharine.

Solomon Horton, Clerk protem

P-61   3RD SATURDAY IN SEPT. 1851

Church met and after preaching proceded to Buisness

1st   Apointed Brother John Givens Moderator for the day

2   Opened a dore for the reception of members

3rd   Caled for the Letter to send to the Association Which Was read and received

4th   Agreed to petition Union, McMinn, Rogers Creek and Goodfield Churches for there Ministerial Ade to Attend At our Sacremental meeting and apointed our Delligates to the Association to bare said petitions.

Thos. Stephens, Church Clerk

3RD FRIDAY BEFORE THE 3RD SATURDAY IN OCTOBER 1851

Church met and After prayer procede to Buisness

1st   Granted Sister Ragan a letter of Dismission then adjorned till Saturday

Met pursuant to Adjorment proced to Buisness &c. Adjorned til Sabbath Met and adjorned till Monday

Met and Adjorned till Tuesday Met acorden to adjournment opened a dore for the Reception of Members and Received by experience Fall Lee and Nick then Adjorned till Wednesday

Met Adjorned tel Thursday at Night opened a dore for the Reception of members and Received by Experience A. J. Chamlee then Adjorned tel friday Met opened a dore for the Reception of Members and Received by Experience Eliza Emaline Chamlee

2 Apointed Breathern John Cunningham, George Stephens, and Thos. Stephens Commishionners to superintend the repars of the Meeting house and

to purchase A stove for the Church

Thos. Stephens, C. C.

N. B. Mary Stephens Deceased Oct.10th 1851 at 8 O'Clock in the evening the Wife of George Stephens (senior)

P-62   3RD SATURDAY IN NOV. 1851

No Meeting

3RD SATURDAY IN DECEMBER 1851

Church met and after Prayer proceded to Buisness

1st Opened a dore for the Reception of Members &c

2nd Received and granted A petition from Bethlehem Churches Requesting of this Church to send our pastor to help ordain S. M. Haun to the Ministry

Signed by order of the Church.

Thos. Stephens, C. C.

3RD SATURDAY IN JANUARY 1852

Church met and After prayer proceded to Buisness

1st Opened a dore for the Reception of Members &c

Thos. Stephens, Church Clerk

P-63   3RD SATURDAY IN MAY 1852

Church met After prayer opened a dore for the reception of members &c. Received and granted a petition from Goodfield by the of Lee Neal

Thos Stephens, C. Clerk

3RD SATURDAY IN JUNE 1852

Church met No Buisness done.

S. Horton, A.C. Clerk

3RD SATURDAY IN JULY 1852

Church met and After preaching proceded to Buisness

1st Opened a dore for the Reception of members

2nd Ordered the Clerk prepare the Letter to send to the Association by Sept. Meeting

3rd Apointed Breathern Wm C. Lee, Thos. Wallis, and Thos. Stephens Delligates to the Association at Ocoee Church Polk County, Tenn

4th Agreed to send by hur Delligates $1.50 to Help Defray the expence of the Association.

Thos. Stephens, Church Clerk

3RD SATURDAY IN AUGUST 1852

No Meeting

Thos Stephens, C. Clerk

3RD SATURDAY IN SEPTEMBER 1852

Church met After preaching proceded to Buisness

1st Opened a dore for the Reception of Members and

2 Received the letter to send to the Association

3rd Agreed to petition Bethlehem, Union, McMinn, Symrna, Rogers Creek, Goodfield and New Friendship Churches to Attend us in Oct. next By there Ministers and Deacons And to Administer the Lord's Supper

4 Agreed to empower our Delligates to the Association to Ask for the next Association in Case no Church ask for it

5 Granted Sister Susannah Rogan a Letter of Dismission

6 Received and Granted a Petition from Bethlehem Requesting Our Minister & Deacons

P-64 By the Request George Stephens the Church released him from being a Commishioner (or agent) and pointed Brother Joseph Sands (Junior) in his stid.

Thos. Stephens, Church Clerk

3RD SATURDAY MARCH, 1853.

Brother Wm Warrick that he had bin drunk and was sorry for it to Which the Church forgave him.

Wm Samuel Ac. Clerk

N. B. March 1853 Brother George Long deceased.

3RD SATURDAY IN APRILE 1853

Church Met and After Prayer preceded to Buisness

1st Opened a dore for the Reception of members

2nd Received and Granted 2 petitions one from N. Hopewell asking for help to ordain a Deacon & to Administer the Lord's supper the other one from New Prospect asking for this Church to attend with them to Consider the propriety of com to a Disolution Whare a po the Church apointed Bretherin James Jarvis, Joseph Sands, Jahew Cunningham and Wm C. Lee to attin said Church

Signed by order of the Church the day above Written

Thos. Stephens, Church Clerk

P-65   SATURDAY JUNE 1853

Church Met and after preaching preceded to Buisness

1st Opened a Dore for the Reception

2ndly Received and granted two petitions for Ministerial & Deacons ade to attend on a Sacremental ocasion one from Goodfield Megs Co. the other one from Bethlehem Monroe Co.

N. B. Sarah Herrell Dec. 18 June 1853 at 3 O'Clock a.m. adjorned

Thos. Stephens, Church Clerk

3RD SATURDAY IN AUGUST 1853

Church met and after preaching proceded to Buisness

1st Opened a dore for the Reception of members

2 Ordered the Clerk to prepare a Letter to send to the Association

3rd Apointed Brother Wm C. Lee Thomas Stephens and James Jarvis Delligates to the Association

4th Agreed to Contribut $1.50 to help Defray Expenses of the Association

5 Impowered the Delligates to the Association to Ask for the next Association in Case no Church ask for it

6th Agreed to petition the following Churches for ade to Attend our sacremental meeting in Oct. next to Wit, Bethlehem Rogers Creek, Smurna Union McMinn, Goodfield and the Loaned Mountain

7 Apointed Brother George Stephens to bare the petition to Bethlehem Broth Wm C. Lee to Union, McMinn and the Delligate to the Association to Bare the Other petition.

Thos. Stephens, Church C.

Sabbath received & granted a petishion from Union, McMinn Church Asking for Ministerial And Deacons Ade to attend them in Sept. 2nd Saturday on a Sacremental Ocasion.

Thos. Stephens, Church Clerk

3RD SATURDAY IN JULY 1854

The Church met and after prayer proceeded to Buisness

1st Opened a Dore for the Reception of members and Received By letter Sister Mary Stephens and Brother Samuel Williams

2nd. Received and granted a petition from Bethlehem Church askin ade to attend A Sacremental Meeting

3rd. Agreed to petition Bethlehem Church for ther preacher to take the Cear of the Church and Apointed Brother George Stephens and Johngh Cunningham to bare said petition

Wm Sampel   A.C. Clerk

P-67   3RD SATURDAY IN NOV. 1854

the Church met and after preaching proceded to Buisness

1st Opened a Dore for the Reception of Members and Received by Letter Catharine Herrell then Adjorned

Thos. Stephens, Church Clerk

3RD SATURDAY IN MAY 1855

the Church met and after prayer proceded to Buisness

1st Opened a Dore for the Reception of members &c

2nd By the information Brother George Stephens the Church brought A Charge Against Brother Wm Warrick for Drunkness and for Fidling and Dancing and After som Consideration of the same the Church Declared and unfellowship Against him.

T. M. Isbill, Moderator

3RD SATURDAY IN OCT. 1855

the Church met and after preaching proceded to buisness

1st Opened a dore for the Reception of members and Received Sister Elizabeth Stephens By Letter and Dismissed by letter Brother Samuel Williams.

Wm Sampel Ac. Clerk

P-68   OCT. 23RD 1855

The Church met and after prayer proceded to buisness

1st Opened a dore for the Reception of members By Experience July Ann Frisby & Mary Renfroe

Wm Sampel Ac. Clerk

MARCH 4TH SABBATH 1856

The Church met And after prayer proceded to Buisness

1st Opened a Dore for the Reception of Members

2 Brother Sollomon Horton And his Wife Nancy Horton Aplied for Letters of Dismission Which Was Granted.

Wm Sampel Ac. Clerk

3RD SATURDAY IN DECEMBER 1855

Church met and after prayer proceded to Buisness

1st Changed Meeting day from the 3rd to 4th Saturday

2nd.   Received Brother Samuel M. Horton to the Pastorial Cear of the Church.

Wm Sampel, Ac. Clerk

4TH SATURDAY IN FEB. 1856

the Church met And After Prayer proceded to Buisness

1st Opened a dore for the Reception of Members

2nd the Church took a Charge Against Brother Seth Walker for Disordy Conduct and Excluded him from the fellowship also the Church took (P-69) a Charge Against Sister Nancy Ray for Disorderly Conduct from Report And not attending Church Meeting and on said Charge Excluded hur from the fellowship of the Church.

Wm B. Sampel Ac. Clerk

4TH SATURDAY IN APRILE 1856

Church Met And after prayer proceded to Buisness

1st Opened a dore for the Reception of members

2 Granted Letters of Dismission to Wm C. Lee Manervy Lee and F. M. Lee

3rd Received and granted a petition from Union, McMinn Church askin Ade of us to Attend a Sacramental Meeting with them in June next then Adjorned.

Thos. Stephens, C. Clerk

4TH SATURDAY IN JUNE 1856

the Church met and after prayer proceded to Buisness

1st Opened a Dore for the Reception of Members And Received Sister Jane Nucom from Madisonville Church by letter.

T. Stephens, C. Clerk

P-70   4TH SATURDAY IN JULY 1856

The Church met And afterpprayer proceded to Buisness

1st   Opened a dore for the Reception of members

2ndly   Apointed a Sacremental Meeting Commencing friday before the 3 Saturday in Oct. next and Agreed to petition the following named Churches for Ade to Wit Union, McMinn, New Providence, Rogers Creek, and Liberty and apointed the Delligate to the Association to bare said petition

3rd   Ordered the Clerk to Write a letter to the Association And have it at next meeting for inspection and apointed Brother James Jarvis Wm Sampel and George Stephens our Delligates to the Association

4   Agreed to send to the Association $1.50 to help Defray Exspenses of the Association.

Thos. Stephens, C. Clerk

4TH SATURDAY IN AUGUST 1856

the Church Met and After prayer proceded to Buisness

1st   Opened a dore for the Reception of members

2nd   Sister Long aplied for a Letter of Dismishion Which Was granted.

3rd   Received the Letter to send to the Association

4   Appointed Brother Joseph Sands and Jomugh Cunningham As Delligates to attend a Convention to Meet at Salem Church, McMinn County (Tenn) on friday before the 4th Saturday in Oct. next in Order to Ratify or Reject a proposition to unight the Baptist Churches again apun the subject of Missionary Efforts And apointed a Committee (P-71) To Draft Suitable Resolution Apun the sd. subject and have it Before the Church at the next meeting for ther Consideration (Committee) Thos. Stephens, James Jarvis, Wm B. Sampel, George Stephens and Johugh Cunningham

Thos Stephens, C. Clerk

FRIDAY BEFORE THE 3RD SATURDAY IN OCT. 1856

Church Met And Adjorned untill Saturday

Met and Chose Brother S. M. Haun and Wm. C. Lee as a Presbytry to set aparte Brothers Johugh Cunningham and James Jarvis to the office of Deacons the presbytry proceded to Discharge the Duties assigned them when on an examination the Brothers Was found Orthodox in faith of the Church And Was set Aparte as Deacons for the Church then Adjorned from day to day untill Saturday in Which time Received Mary West by Exsperance then opened a dore for the Reception of Members and Received Mary Ann Taylor, Sarah Caroline Weathers, T. I. Johnson, S. H. Hubbard, Huston Cunningham and Thomas Barber by Exsperance   then Adjorned untill evening

Met pursuant to adjornment   opening a dore for the Reception of Members and Received by Exsperance John H. Cunningham, Eleas Kerby, Sarah Kerby Matilda Hartley, Benjamin Hartley, Harvy H. Brown, Harriette Stephens and Sousann Brown Also Received Johugh Hitower and his Wife Rebecca Hitower as by Letter — then adjorned

Thos. Stephens, Church Clerk

P-73   3RD SATURDAY IN NOV. 1856

Church Met and After prayer opened a dore for the Reception of members And received by Exsperance George A. Stephens, Samson Stephens, Wm Covell, Wm Kerby Rebecca Stephens, Easter E. Smith, Mary Stephens, Susannah McTankford, Liza Hitower Bartlett West, Hazel Harrell and James Weathers And then Dismissed by Letter Sister Nancy Warrick

Saturday night Received by Exsperance Catharine Ballanger & Sarah McDaniel Monday night the Church recinded the Act of the Church Declaring unfellowship Against Brother John Hitower and Admits him to the fellowship of the Church Received by exsperance Julia, a Woman of Coller belonging to Jos Walker, Tuesday Received as by Letter Albert Grayson and Mary Proffet and Nancy Nucom By Exsperance Wednesday Received Jain Gill by Exsperance Also Received Mallinda a Woman of Coller belonging to John Cunningham by Exsperance thursday Received by Exsperance Bayler, a man of culler belonging to Joseph Cunningham then adjorned.

Thos. Stephens, C. Clerk

4TH SATURDAY IN DECEMBER 1856

tha Church met and after preaching opened a dore for the Reception of members and received by Exsperance James Jarvis, Luke Frisby John Stephens, Harell Herrill, Samuel Thomas Harrison Jarvis Bayte Frisby John A man of culler belonging to Bayts Carter, Licissa, a Woman of Culler belonging to Wilson Weathers Also Received as by letter   (P-74) H. W. Herrell by Exsperance Sarah Ballinger, Me C. Harrell & Saturday night Received Thomas A. Dorithy by Exsperance, Sister N. J. Dorithy as by letter, F. C. Tucker and his Wife H. Tucker as by letter, and Elizabeth Nucom, Wm Land and his Wife Jane Land by Exsperance, Nemrod Lunsford as by Letter. Monday received Georgia Jarvis by Exsperance Teusday Night Received Huston Cunningham, Curtis Gill Robert M. Stephens, and Wm A. F. Stephens by Exsperance Wednesday Received John Fergerson and his Wife Catharine Fergerson By Exsperance then Adjorned

Thos Stephens, C. Clerk

4TH SATURDAY IN JANUARY 1857

Church met opened A dore for the Reception of members, None Received.

T. Stephens, C. Clerk

4TH SATURDAY IN FEBRUARY 1857

Church Met and After prayer proceded to Buisness

1st Opened a Dore for the Reception of members then Adjorned till Evening then Met acordan to adjornment opening a dore for the Reception of members and Received by exsperance Mary Ann Barker, Nancy Catharine Randolph, Sheby Hitower and Sarah Hitower, then Adjorned

Met Sabbath Eving and Received by Exsperance Reubin Kerby and his Wife Kerby, Thomas Harrell and --- . . . Harmon By request of Sister Nancy Warrick the Act granted hur letter is resinded.

T. Stephens, C. Clerk

P-75 ## 4TH SATURDAY IN MARCH 1857

Church Met And after prayer proceded to Buisness

1st Opened a dore for the Reception of members and received E. Hensley by Exsperance

4TH SATURDAY IN APRILE 1857

Church Met And After prayer proceded to Buisness

1st Opened a dore for the Reception of members and Received Hickman by Letter

2 Apointed Brother T. Stephens and James Jarvis to attend at Goodfield Church in Convention With other Churches apon the subject of our boundary line between us and Sweetwater and Hiwassee Associations.

T. Stephens, Clerk

4TH SATURDAY IN MAY 1857

4TH SATURDAY IN JUNE 1857

Church Met And after prayer proceded to Buisness

1st   Opened a dore for the Reception of Members And Received by Letter R. C. Blackwell

2   Received a petition from Nochey Creek Church praying for ade to Help Settle A diffrance between hur and Bethlehem Church Whare a pon the Church Apointed Breathern T. Stephens, James Jarvis, John Cunningham And Jos Sands to attend With their Churches as helps

P-76   then Adjorned untill Evning

Met pursuant to Adjornment And Received by Exsperance N. Kerby and Milley Harmon then Adjorned tell Sabbath Morning then met and Received by Letter Jacob Williams and his Wife and then Adjorned.

T. Stephens, C. Clerk

4TH SATURDAY IN JULY 1857

Church met and after prayers proceded to Buisness

1st   Opened a dore for the Reception of members & Apointed a sacremental meeting Commencing on friday before the 1st Saturday in Oct. next and agreed to petition the following Churches for Aid to Wit Pisga Shoal Creek, Ocoee And apointed John Fergusen, R. M. Stephens and George Stephens to bare the petition Ordered the Clerk to Write the letter to send to the Association And Apointed Breathern Wm B. Sampel, John Fergarson and George Stephens to Report to us in the Association And in Case of failure T. Stephens or Johugh Cunningham be their alternate.

3rd Agreed to Contribute $2.00 to help Defray the Exspense of the Association.

T. Stephens, C. Clerk

4TH SATURDAY IN AUGUST 1857

Church Met and After Prayer proceded to Buisness Opened a dore for the Reception of members.

2nd   Received Received the Letter to send to the Association

3rd   Apointed Breathern Thos Stephens and Wm B. Sampel to Attend a Convention Meeting of Baptistist to meet   (P-77)   With Salem Church, McMinn Co., Tenn. on friday before the 4th Saturday in Oct. next (Apun the subject of a Union)

4th Sister, Hickman, Reuben Kirby, Casity Kirby, Nancy Kirby, Millie Harmon, Nancy Harmon and - - - - - - Kirby Aplied for Letters of Dismission Which Was Granted   then Adjorned untill Evning.

Met pursuant to Adjormmen opened a dore for the Reception of

Members

2nd the Church agreed to Receive the Acts And Doings of the Convention Which met With Goodfield Church in May last.

T. Stephens, C. Clerk

4TH SATURDAY IN SEPTEMBER

No meeting

FRIDAY BEFORE THE 1st SATURDAY IN OCT. 1857

Church met and after prayer proceded to Buisness

1st Opened a Dore for the Reception of Members

2nd the Church took a Charge against Brother Elyas Kirby for lying And after some Consideration the Church declared an unfellowship to him (or Against him) then Adjorned till Saturday

Met pursuant to adjornment

1st Opened a Dore for the Reception of Members

2nd Brother Johngh Hitower And Sister Rebeca Hitower, Brother E. P. Tucker and Sister Harriette Tucker aplied for Letters of Dismission Which Was granted them. Adjorned.

P-78   4TH SATURDAY IN NOVEMBER 1857

Deaths of members in the A. D. 1857 &8:

Sarah Hitower
Catharine Herrill
Polly Ann Barker

FRIDAY BEFORE THE 4TH SATURDAY IN DECEMBER 1857

Church met and after preaching proceded to Buisness

1st Opened a dore for the Reception of members

2nd By the information of Brother George Stephens the Church took a Charge Against Sister Susannah McTankford for Ludeness and spon sd Charge the Church Excludes hur from the fellowship of the Church

3rdly the Church Apointed Breathern Johugh Cunningham And
A. I. Chamlee, Elijah McDaniel, George Stephens and Joseph Sands (Junior)
A Comitee to investigate the Conduct of Sister Nick. the Comitee Retirred
And in a few Minutes the Comitee returned And advised the Church to take
a Charge Against Sister Nick for Ludeness And apon said Charge the Church
Excludes her from the fellowship of the Church, then the Church Adjorned.

T. Stephens, Clerk

P-79   4TH SATURDAY IN JANUARY 1858

the Church met and after prayer proceded to Buisness

4TH SATURDAY IN FEB. 1858

The Church met and after preaching proceded to Buisness

1st Opened a dore for the Reception of members

2nd the Church Agreed to Delligate to the Convention Meeting
of Baptists to meet With the Mt. Pleasant Church in May next and apointed
Breathern Johugh Cunningham and James Jarvis as Delligates to sd meeting
which meeting is to effect a union iff possible

3rd the Church agreed to Receive the preasant propisition as
the Basis of the Union (See) Convention Minnet of 1857)

Ordered the Clerk to prepare the letter for sd meeting

Received Sister Mary Jones by letter

Thos. Stephens, Church Clerk

Samuel M. Haun, Moderator

4TH SATURDAY IN MARCH 1858

The Church Met and After preaching proceded to Buisness

1st Opened a dore for the Reception of Members then Adjorned
untill Evning Met pursuant to adjornment and Received Sister M. C. Snider
by Letter then Adjorned untill Sabbath

Met pursuant to Adjornment untill Sabbath Met pursuant to Adjornment And Recvd by Letter Parshal W. Cate.

Thos. Stephens,
Church Clerk

4TH SATURDAY IN JUNE

Church Met and after prayer proceded to Buisness

1st   Opened a dore for the reception of members

2nd   Agreed to have a sacremental Meeting on friday before the 4th Saturday in Oct. next Agreed to petition the following Churches for ade to Wit, Pisga, Shoal Creek, Smyria, Bethlehem, and Ocose and Apointed R. M. Stephens, George Jarvis, Jahugh Cunningham, J. Jarvis, T. Stephens H. Cunningham and S. Stephens to bare petition then adjorned till Sabbath Recvd by exsperance, A man of Coller belonging to Wm Spenser.

Thos. Stephens, C. Clerk

4TH SATURDAY IN JULY 1858

Church Met and After prayer proceded to Buisness

1st   Opened a dore for the Reception of members

2nd   Ordered the Clerk to Write the Letter to send to the Association And Apointed Breathern Thos. Stephens, James Jarvis and P. E. Cate to bare the same

3   Brother A. J. Chamlee & his Wife, E. C. Chamlee aplied for letters of Dismission Which Was granted

T. Stephens, C. Clerk

4TH SATURDAY IN AUGUST 1858

Church Met and After prayer proceded to buisness

1st   Opened A dore for the Reception of members

2   Caled for the letter to send to the Association Which Was Red and Recvd.

P-81   ### 4TH SATURDAY IN SEPT. 1858

Church Met And After preaching proceded to Business

1st   Apointed Brother T. M. Isbill Moderator for the day.

2nd   Opened a dore for the reception of members

3rd   Agreed to Continue our former delligation to the Convention at Sweetwater to Wit, T. Stephens and J. Laws Without making any change in the proposition for a Union.

T. M. Isbill, Md.
T. Stephens, C. Clerk

FRIDAY BEFORE THE 4TH SATURDAY IN OCT. 1858

Church met And after preaching proceded to Buisness

1st Opened A dore for the reception of members –

Saturday Met – Sabbath Met – Monday Met – Tuesday met – And at night Recvd by exsperance Samuel Ously Wm Hare and Mary Ingram and by letter Brother James & Sister Harriette of Coller belonging to Friend Creaghead

T. Stephens, C. Clerk

4TH SATURDAY IN NOV. 1858

Church met and after prayer proceded to Business

1st Opened a dore for the Reception of Members

2nd Agreed to sell the Old Meeting house And Apointed Breathern T. Stephens and Jas Walker sold it either at public or private sale and that they report there sale to the Church When sold

3rd Brother Wm Cavel Aplied for a Letter of Dismission Which Was granted.

T. Stephens, C. Clerk

P-82   FRIDAY BEFORE THE 4TH SATURDAY IN DECEMBER 1858

Church met and after prayer proceded to Buisness Opened a dore for the reception of members and received Sister as by Letter then Adjorned tell Saturday Met pursuant to Adjornment First opened a dore for the Reception of members

2 Brother George Stephens (Treasury for the Church) Reports six Dollars in his hand whar a pon the Church Ordered him to pay it over to Thos. Stephens and Joseph Walker (Building Committee Which Was don

3 By motion of Brother Thos Stephens it was Resolved unanimously that the Church feel thankful for to John Ray the gift to a pease of Land for the Benefit of the Church (See Title Papers Registered in Book

A, Page 90, Dated Sept. 14th 1858.

Thos Stephens, Clerk
S. M. Haun, Md.

4TH SATURDAY IN JAN. 1859

Church Met and After Preaching proceded to Buisness

2nd Apointed Harrison Jarvis protem Clk opened a dore for the Reception of members

3 A Charge Was Brought by the Church Against the following members for dancing to Wit, Hazel Harrell, H. H. Brown, John W. Walker, and Mary Ann West Also a Charge Against Boby a man of Coller belonging to Jas Cunningham for Drunkness and apon sd Charges the Church Excludes them from hur fellowship then Sister Mary Profit and W. Sheets & Pheby Ann Sheets, applied for Letters of Dismission Which Was Granted.

T. Stephens, C. Clerk

Polly Hitower Departed this lefe Feb. 16th 1859 the Wife of John Hitower

P-83   4TH SATURDAY IN FEBRUARY 1859

Church met and after preaching proceded to Buisness

1st Opened a dore for the Reception of Members

2nd the Church Brought A Charge against Wm for swarring and apon sd Charge excludes him from hur fellowship

3rd the Church Brought a Charge by Broth. C. L. Hensley Against July a slave belonging to J. L. Walker for Ludeness and apon sd Charge Excludes hur from the fellowship of the Church, then Adjorned till Evning Opening a dore for the Reception of members And Recvd Only a slave belonging to George Stephens by Exsperance then adjorned.

Thos. Stephens, C. Clerk

4TH SATURDAY IN MARCH 1859

Church Met And After preaching proceded to Buisness

1st Opened a Dore for the Reception of members &c.

Thos Stephens, C. Clerk

4TH SATURDAY IN APRILE 1859

Church met and after preaching proceded to Buisness

1st Apointed T. M. Isbill, Moderator for the day

2nd Opened A dore for the Reception of members

3rd Their being a consel meeting to be helt at Mt. Pleasant Church it Was Agreed that as many of this Church as Wants to partisapate in sd meeting to do so

N. B. Johugh Cunningham Deceased May 3rd 1859 (Deacon)

N. B. Polly Stephens Departed this Life May 15th 1859 (Daughter of S. Stephens)

N. B. George A. Stephens Deceased June 25th 1859

P-84   4TH SATURDAY MAY 1859

Church met And After preaching proceded to buisness

1st Opened a Dore for the Reception of members

2nd Received and Granted a petition from Citico Church Whare a pon the Church Apointed Breathern James Jarvis and Thos. Stephens to attend with sd Church as Requested.

4 Granted a Letter of Dismission to Sister Sarah Williams.

                              Elijah McDaniel,
                              Clerk protem

                    4TH SATURDAY IN JUNE 1859

Church met and no buisness done.

                              Thos. Stephens, C. Clerk

                    4TH SATURDAY IN JULY 1859

Church met And after preaching proceded to Buisness

1st Opened a Dore for the Reception of members

2nd the Church apointed Breathern James Jarvis & Thos Stephens to attend a Convention Meeting of Baptists to meet With the Sweetwater Church apon the subject of Union

3rd.   Ordered the Clerk to prepare a Letter to send it to the Association by next meeting for inspection And apointed Thos. Stephens & James Jarvis to bare the same to the Association as Delligates

4th Church agrees to send $1.50 to help Defray the Exspense of the Association

5 Agreed to pettition Union McMinn, New Providence and Shoal Creek Churches for Ministerial and Deacons Ade to attend on a Sacramental ocasion to Come off in Oct. 4th Saturday. Apointed George Stephens, R. M. Stephens and Wm A. F. Stephens to bare the petitions.

T. Stephens, Church Clerk

P-85   FRIDAY BEFORE THE 4TH SATURDAY IN DECEMBER 1859

Church at Christianburg Met and after preaching proceded to Buisness

1st Opned a dore for the Reception of members

2nd Caled to the letter to send to the Consul Meeting at this place there being no letter prepared it Was agreed that John Hitower and Samson Stephens should Attend the same Without Letter. Adjorned till Saturday 11 O'Clock Met pursuant to Adjornment After preaching proceded to Buisness

1st Opened A Dore for the Reception of members

2nd Chosed Breathern (Elder) Z. Rose and S. M. Haun as a presbytry to set apart Brother Samson Stephens as a Deacon for this Church and after the Examination the presbytry pronounced sd Brother sound in the faith of the Church And Was set aparte as Deacon for sd Church

3rd Apointed Brothers James Jarvis, Huston Cunningham, and Thomas A. Dorithy Commissioners to settle with the building Committee of the Church And that they report ther action to the church then Adjorned till Sabbath 11 O'Clock met pursuant to Adjornment And Apointed A protracted meeting Commencing friday before the 1st Saturday in Nov. next and that Z. Rose With the paster attend the same.

Thos. Stephens, C. Clerk

4TH SAT. IN JAN. 1860

Church met and after preaching proceded to Buisness

1st Opned a dore for the Reception of members

2nd   Granted Sister M. J. Thomas A Letter of Dismission

Thos. Stephens, C. Clerk

4TH SAT. IN FEBRUARY 1860

Church at Christianburg Met And after preaching proceded to Buisness

1st   Opened a Dore for the Reception   (P-86)   And Recvd by Exsperance Mary Cate

2   The Commissioners Apointed to settle with the Building Committee Ask Leave to Report their settlement with sd. Building Committee

1.   We find that thay have Collected off of the public including themselves the sum of $662.55

2   Thay have expended sum of $648.04

3   Leaving in their hands the sum of $14.51

4   We find on Superscription the sum of $63.50 Which may be collected

5   Also on same paper the sum of .31 Which is in a Condition that Cannot be Collected

6   We find the building Jas Walker & Thos. Stephens in debt to James Montgomery in the sum of 150 with interest 2 years.

7   We also find the sd. Walker and Stephens Bound to fense the Burial ground

8   There is 2 other items of Exspence to Wit. the Panting of the Windows Blinds and the underpending of the Meeting house all of Which is submitted this the 11th day of Feb. 1860

F. A. Dority
Huston Cunningham
James Jarvis

3.   The Church after the Above report Was submitted for the Consideration Agreed to beare the Building Commitee Harmless And undertook to Assom the Debt.

4.   Auterize the sd. Walker And Stephens to go on and Complete the house And Burial Ground.

Don in Church Conferance the date Above Written

S. M. Haun, Moderator
T. Stephens, Clerk

P-87   4TH SATURDAY IN MARCH 1860

            Church met at Christianburg and After preaching proceded to
buisness

            1st Opened a Dore for the Reception of members

            2 Recvd a petition from Big Spring Church Askin helps to go
to Pisga Church to Help Settle a Difficulty in Pisga Church and After some
Consideration of the same Agreed to Lay it over until next Meeting in Corse

            Recvd by Letter Elizabeth Ingram

                                        Thos. Stephens, C. Clerk

                    4TH SATURDAY IN APRILE 1860

            Church Met And After preaching proceded to buisness

            1st Opened a dore for the reception of members And received
by Letter Winney and Nancy Renfroe and also Mary Warrick by letter Received by exsperance Elizabeth and Margaret Warrick

            2nd Brothers Jos. Walker and Thomas Stephens Ask leave to re-
port to the Church that thay have sold the Old Meeting house for $20 Whare
a pon the Church Confirms the sale of the same

            3 Caled up the refferance from last meeting in Refferance to
Delligating to Pisga Church and after some remarks the Church Delligates
to said Meeting and Apointed Brothern John Hitower and Thomas Stephens
there Delligates to sd. meeting.

                                        Thos. Stephens, C. Clerk

            At night received Mary Proffitt by letter

                    4TH SATURDAY IN MAY 1860

            Church met and after prayer proceded to Buisness

            N. C. Received by Letter Mary Proffitt & Sister Ingram

P-88   4TH SATURDAY IN JUNE 1860

            Church met and after preaching proceded to Buisness

            1st Opned a Dore for the Reception of members

2 the Church Brought a Charge Against Brother Curtis Gill for Drunkness and apointed Brothers Huston Cunningham and Elijah McDaniel to notify Brother Gill of the same by next meeting

At night received a man of coller belonging to Joseph Walker by exsperance

Thos. Stephens, C. Clerk

4TH SATURDAY IN JULY 1860

Church met and after prayer proceded to Buisness

1st Apointed Brother Gwin Wallis Moderator for this meeting

2 Opned a dore for the reception of members

3 Caled up the Refference against brother C. Gill Brother Gill being presant gave the Church satisfaction whare a pon the Church forgave him

4 Ordered the Clerk to Write a Letter to send to the Association and Apointed Brothers John Fergerson and Thos. Stephens to bare the same and in Case of falur Brother H. Cunningham suply

5. Agreed to send up $1.50 to Help Defray Exspences of the Association.

Thos. Stephens, C. Clerk

4TH SATURDAY IN AUGUST 1860

Church met and after prayer proceded to buisness

1st Apointed Brother Jacob Williams Moderator

2 Opned a Dore for the Reception of members

3 Asked the Association to Reconsider there Act of 1837 in referance to there DeClaration of non fellowship And the Withdrawal Resolution from Churches &c

P-89 4 Also Apointed a Union Meeting to Commence on Friday before the 4th Saturday in July 1861 and Asked the Association to send Ministerial Aid to attend the same

5 Caled for the letter to send to the association Red and Recvd by adding the name of Brother Joseph Sands as a Delligate to the Association.

Thos. Stephens, C. Clerk.

4TH SATURDAY IN SEPT. 1860

Church met and after preaching proceded to Buisness

1st Apointed Brother James Jarvis (Junior) Clerk for the day

2 Opned a dore for the Reception of members

3rd the Church Brought A Charge Against Brothers Lunsford for failing to attend his meeting and also for joining the Methodist Society and excludes him from the fellowship of the Church.

4th Agreed to take the Lord's Supper on the 1st Sabbath in Nov. next and agreed to petition the following Churches for ministerial and Deacons Ade to Wit: Notchey Creek Mt. Pleasant, and Union, McMinn Churches for ads

5 Apointed Parshal W. Cate, Samson Stephens and John Fergerson & H. Cunningham bare sd petitions.

6 Brother James Jarvis Caled for a Letter of Dismission for himself and his Wife Which Was granted Brother Samuel Ousley Caled for a letter of Dismission Which Was Granted them. Adjorned till Evning Met pursuant to Adjornment Opned a Dore for the Reception of members and Received by Exsperance Mary Thomas, Henry Cartwright and John Stephens The last named Who became dissatisfied beleving that when he Was first Baptised he had no Gods in his sole then Adjorned.

James L. Jarvis, Assistant
Clerk

P-90   FRIDAY BEFORE THE FIRST SATURDAY IN NOV. 1860

Church met and after preaching proceded to Buisness

1st Opened a dore for eht Reception of members

2. The Church Chose Brother John Fergerson to act as Deavon (Iff found Orthodox in faith and practice) then Adjorned till Saturday

Met pursuant to Adjornment And proceded to Buisness By Choising (Elders) Z. Rose, and S. M. Haun presbytry to examine Brother Fergerson And a pon Examination by sd presbytry He Was found Orthodox Andset aparte to the office of Deacon for the Church Then Adjorned til evning

Met And Recvd Nancy McBride by Recantation then Adjorned till Sabbath Recvd By Letter Miram T. Stephens and Dismissed by letter P. W. Cate & Mary Cate then adjorned from day to day untill the next Sabbath And Recvd by Exsperance Levi Nucom, Mary Nucom, Elijah Nucom, E. Nucom, Jeremiah Williams and Isaac Ingram by reCantation and by exsperance Nancy Fore, Crockette Nucom, Elizabeth Cunningham And by Recantation Harry Brown by Exsperance Thos Emless, T. O. Herrill, B. Hunt, T. Hunt, I. Nucom, M. Nucom, Dan Nucom, S. Williams, O. Sneed, I. Lane, M. Renfroe, R. A. Webb, Matilda Herrell, H. Roy, A. Sneed And received by letter Wm Nucom, Elizabeth Nucom Fanny Nucom, Matilda Blokely, and William A. Cartwright.

Thos. Stephens, Clerk

4TH SATURDAY IN DECEMBER 1860

Church met and after preaching proceded to Buisness

1st Opned a dore for the reception of members

P-91   2nd the Church Brought a Charge Against Brother Curtis Gill for Drunkness And using profane language andafter some Consideration the Church Declared unfellowship to him, then Adjorned till Evning Met and Recvd by Exsperance Elizabeth Williams

Thos. Stephens, Clerk

4TH SATURDAY IN JANUARY 1861

4TH SATURDAY IN FEBRUARY 1861

Church Met And After preaching proceded to Buisness

1st Opning A dore for the Reception of members

2nd Dismissed by Letter Wilber Sheets, and Wife, A. J. Sneed, and Wife And Mary Profit

T. Stephens, Clerk

Saturday Evning Recvd by Exsperance A. J. Presley

P-92   AUGUST 4TH SATURDAY

(Or During the Spring & fall fhe following Acount taken, the Clerk not keeping up his servases or records Monthly)

Dismissed by letter Wm F.,Elizabeth and D. C. Nucoms By Letter Elizabeth Barnett By letter Recvd by letter Wm, Sally, Malissa, & Mary Jain Crofferds.

Apointed Thos. Stephens, John Fergerson & Samson Stephens Delligates to the Association Ordered the Clerk to prepare the letter to the Association and present at next meeting for inspection

Sept. the letter Received

4TH SAT. IN OCT. 1861

John McBride Recvd by letter

FRIDAY BEFORE THE 4TH SATURDAY IN OCT. 1861

Church met and After preaching proceded to Buisness

1st Opning a dore for the reception of members

2nd Caled up the Refferance Against the two sisters Ann & Wassie for using profain languge And After hearing the testimony Against them the Church excluded them from hur fellowship

3rd the Church preferred a Charge Against George Herrill for Contempt in refusing to Com forred & give the Church satisfaction in relation to fighting with the boys

4th Apointed Brothers F. & T. Stephens to notify him of the Charge then Adjorned till evning. Met pursuant to adjornment Caled up the refferance Against George Herrell And Declared unfellowship to him then Adjorned till Sabbath.

Then met and adjorned from day to day untill the next Sabbath in Which tim the Church (P-93) Recvd by letter sister Ann Kile and Mary Hitower. Recvd the following persons in to hur fellowship to Wit

By Exsperance

      A. Gun
      Mary Williams
      Cornelia Crawford
      Jain Barnett
      E. C. Herd
      Susan Ingram
      Nancy Williams
      Matilda West
      Elizabeth Ingram
      George Kile
      Wm F. Thurman
      Mary Herd
      Catherine Gun
      Harriett Nucom
      Hamilton Crawford
      Sara Isabel Herrill
      John D. Dixon
      A Woman of color belonging to John Rowan and
Elizabeth Kile by letter. Then Adjorned till 4th Saturday in Nov. next.

                Thomas Stephens, Clerk

4TH SATURDAY IN NOV. 1861

Church Met and after preaching proceded to Buisness

1st opned a Dore for the Reception of members

2 the Church Brought a Charge Against Brother E. C. Herd for swaring and giting Drunk and after Hearing the Evidence Against him Declared unfellowship With him, then Adjorned.

T. Stephens, Clerk

4TH SATURDAY IN DECEMBER 1861

The Church met and after preaching proceded to Buisness

1st Opned a dore for the Reception of members

2 the Church took a Charge Against Brother C. L. Hensley for Drunkness & swaring And after hearing the testimony Against him the Church excludes him from the fellowship of the Church, then Adjorned.

T. Stephens, Clerk

P-94 ### 4TH SATURDAY IN JANUARY L1862

Church Met And after preaching proceded to Buisness

1st Opned a dore for the Reception of members and Recvd C. L. Nucom by Exsperance then adjorned.

T. Stephens, Clerk

4TH SATURDAY IN FEB. 1862

The Church met and after preaching proceded to Buisness

1st opning a dore for the Reception of members

2 Brother Wm Crafferd Caled for letters of dismission for himself and Sally Crofferd, Malisa Crofferd, Mary Jain Crofferd, Carmelia Crofferd & Hamilton Crofferd Which was granted.

3rd the Church took a Charge Against sister Nucom for Leudness and after hearing testimony Against hur the Church Excludes hur from hur fellowship

4th the Church took a Charge Against Brother Thos. Barker by the information of Sister Sheets for attempting to go to Bed to her Without hur concent (In a slandering manner) And after some consideration of

the same the Church Apointed A Committee to Meet with the parties of the
Meeting house between this and next meeting and that they reporte to the
Church the Committee Named

> John McBride
> Huston Cunningham
> Elijah McDaniel
> Wm Sampel
> Joseph Sands

then adjorned

T. Stephens, Clerk

4TH SATURDAY IN MARCH 1862

Church Met and After preaching proceded to Buisness

1st opned a dore for the Reception of members

P-95   2nd Caled up the referance against Brother T. Barker And owing
to the Committee Not being abel to Reporte the Case Was layed over untill
next meeting And that the Committee is Requested to Reporte ther Action
at the next meeting in Corse   then Adjorned.

T. Stephens, Clerk

4TH SATURDAY IN APRILE 1862

Church Met and After preaching proceded to Buisness

1st Caled up the Refferance Against Brother T. Barker and After
some Consideration the Church layed it over untill next meeting on acount
of the Committee not being abel to Report The Committee is Requeste to
Continue ther investigation and that they Report next meeting

3 The Church Apointed Brother John McBride & Elijah McDaniel
to notify the parties to attend next Meeting

3 Brother John Fergerson is Apointed to notify Brother George
Stephens & Wm Fore to attend next meeting as witnesses in the above named
case.

4 Sister Rachel Blackwell aplied for a letter of dismission
which was granted

5 The Church brought a charge Against Sister Susan Brown for
Ludeness And After hearing the evidence against hur the Church excludes
hur from the fellowship of the Church then Adjoned.

T. Stephens, Clerk

4TH SATURDAY IN MAY 1862

Church at Christianburg met and after preaching proceded to Buisness

1st Opned a Dore for the Reception of Members

2 Caled up the Referance Against Brother Thos. Barker the Committee not being abel to Report the Committee Was discharged   (P-96) and After some Consideration the Church droped the Charge against him for Contempt to the Church in Refusing to Com forred to the Church, After being notified to do so to give satisfaction in Relation to the Charge Brought Against him at the Feb. session 1862 and Apointed Brother John McBride to notify him of the same.

T. Stephens, C. Clerk

4TH SATURDAY IN JUNE 1862

The Church at Christianburg Met and After preaching proceded to Buisness

1st opned a dore for the Reception of members

2nd Caled up the Refferance Against Brother T. Barker. Brother Barker not being preasant Brother McBride stated he had notified him to Attend Whar a pon A Mosion Was made and 2nd to terne him out of the Church & Exclude him from hur fellowship.

T. Stephens, C. Clerk

4TH SATURDAY IN JULY 1862

The Church Met and After preaching proceded to Buisness

1st Opned a Dore for the Reception

2nd. Ordered the Clerk to prepare A letter to the Association And have it at next meeting for inspection

3rd Apointed Breathern Thos Stephens, Wm. B. Sampels and John Hitower Our Delligates to the Association And in Case of failure of either of the ones Apointed to Attend Brother Samson Stephens to suply, then Adjorned

T. Stephens, Clerk

4TH SATURDAY IN AUGUST 1862

Church met and after preaching proceded to Buisness

Caled the Church to order

 1st Agreed to petitioning the following Churches for ther Deacon's ade to attend us on friday before the 4th Saturday in Oct. next A Sacremental occasion to Wit, Mt. Pleasant & Union, McMinn And Apointed Breathern John Fergerson and Samson Stephens to bare sd petitions.

        T. Stephens, Clerk

 Henry W. Cartwright Deceased

   FRIDAY BEFORE THE 4TH SATURDAY IN OCT. 1862

 Church Met And met from day to day untill Sabbath Weak and in said time recvd by Exsperance Nucom Hitower and Randolph then Adjorned untill meeting in Corse

        T. Stephens, Clerk

 J. R. Lane, deceased

    4TH SATURDAY IN NOV. 1862

 Church met and After prayer proceded to Buisness

 1st opned A Dore for the Reception of Members and Recvd Francis A. Shelton by Exsperance.

        T. Stephens, Clerk

 Sister Barnette deceased

   THURSDAY BEFORE THE 4TH SATURDAY IN DECEMBER 1862

 Church met And after preaching proceded to Buisness opned a dore for the Reception of members then Adjorned And met from day to day untill Sabbath and Recvd by letter Sister Nancy Lane. then Adjorned.

        Thos. Stephens, Clerk

 Isaac Ingram Died at Vicksburg
 Nancy Warrick , Deceased
 Winney Renfroe, Deceased
 A. J. Presley, Deceased at Vicksburg

    4TH SATURDAY IN MARCH 1863

Church met and After preaching proceded to Buisness

1st   opned a Dore for the Reception of members &c

T. Stephens, C. Clerk

4TH SATURDAY IN APRILE 1863

The Church me t and after preaching proceded to Buisness

1st Chois Brother T. Russell Md. for the day

2nd Opned A Dore for the Reception of Members

T. Stephens, C. Clerk

4TH SATURDAY IN MAY 1863

The Church met and after preaching no further business Done

T. Stephens, C. Clerk

4TH SATURDAY IN JUNE 1863

Church Met and After preaching opning a dore for the Reception of Members No other Buisness done.

T. Stephens, Clerk

4TH SATURDAY IN JULY 1863.

Church me t and after preaching proceded to Buisness

1st opning a Dore for the Reception of members and Restored E. C. Hured to the fellowship of the Church

2nd Apointed Brothers Wm B. Sampel, & John Hitower Building Committee in the Room of Brother H. W. Herrell, resigned and Brother Joseph Walker deceased

T. Stephens, Clerk

P-99   ### 4TH SATURDAY IN MARCH 1864

No Business done.

T. Stephens, Clerk

4TH SATURDAY IN MAY 1864

No Buisness done.

T. Stephens, Clerk

4TH SATURDAY IN JUNE 1864

No Buisness Done.

T. Stephens, Clerk

4TH SATURDAY IN JULY 1864

Church met and After preaching proceded to Buisness

1st Received by Exsperance Landers

4TH SATURDAY IN AUGUST 1864

Church met and after prayer the Church Agreed to Delligate to the Association And Apointed T. Stephens, Joseph Sands and Wm B. Sampels Delligates to the Association

T. Stephens, Clerk

4TH SATURDAY IN SEPT. 1864

Church Met And After preaching Adjorned until Sabbath Met pursuant to Adjornment opned a dore for the reception of members And Recvd Mary Jain Kile And Sarah Cunningham on a Certificate of those being Baptised by a Regular Baptist

Attest

T. Stephens, Clerk,
S. M. Haun Md.

P-100   4TH SATURDAY IN OCT. 1864

Church met and after preaching proceded to Buisness

1st Opned a dore for the Reception of members And Adjorned from Day to Day Untill Sabbath day Week and in sd time transacted the following buisness

Recvd by Exsperance:

Colombus Johnston
J. C. Harris
Robert Harrell
Margaret Stephens,
Margaret Herrell
√ H. Davis
K. Vineyard
M. Vineyard
H. Nucom
Sarah Weathers
E. Johnston
N. McDaniel
S. A. Smith
E. Snider
E. Williams
Frank Herrell
M. Foshee
James M. Herd

Certified C. Vine Yard, Restored James W. Hitower to the fellowship of the Church Who was a member of New Providence and apon evidence of members tbf this Church say he was Excluded Wrongfully

Dismissed by letter C. Johnston And Hambrick

T. Stephens, Clerk
S. M. Haun, Md.

R. M. Stephens Departed this life

4TH SATURDAY IN NOVEMBER 1864

Church met and after preaching proceded to Buisness

1st Chose Brother A. Haun Md for the day A. McDaniel Clerk protem. No Other Buisness done.

E. McDaniel

4TH SATURDAY IN DECEMBER 1864

No Business done

JAN. 1865 UNTIL AUGUST 1865

the following buisness done

Dismissed by letter Brother Wm Fore and his Wife Also Wm Thurman

Sarah Weathers, Deceased

P-101   Total number of members in the Church 176

4TH SATURDAY IN AUGUST 1865

Christianburg Church met After preaching proceded to Buisness

1st Opned a Dore for the Reception of members

2 Apointed Breathern Thomas Stephens, Joseph Sands, Samson Stephens, Delligate to the Association And in cas of failure E. Hurde to suply. Caled on the Clerk to read the letter to the Association Which Was Done & R_ecvd

3rd the Church Amended the Compend:

1. Faith Artickel. We believe in one onely true and living God the fathers Word and holy Gost and that these 3 are one

2. We believe that the Scriptures of the old and new testaments are the word of God and are the only purfick rule of faith and practest

3. We believe in election Accorden to the foreknowledge of God the father through the sanctification of the spirit and belief of the truth

4 Wee believe that by nature wee wars dead in tresspass And sins Children of Wrath eaven as others and as such unabel to Justify ourselves in the sight of God by Any human effort, hence we are Justified freely by Gods grase through the Redemption that is in Christ Jesus.

5. Wee believe in the perserverance and final salvation of all Gods children

6. Wee believe that Baptism is and ordinance of the Church of Jesus Christ and that true believers are the onely proper subjects of sd Ordinance And that the scriptural mode is by immersion

7. Wee believe that the lords supper is Also and Ordinance of the Church of Christ And that thoes onely Who has ben scripturally Baptised and sustains And Accredited membership in sd Church are proper Communicants

8. Wee believe in the Reserection of the dead general Judgment and that the wicked will be adjudged to everlasting punishment And the Rightous to Life Eternal

P-103   9. Wee believe that no minister of the Gospel has a right to Administer the Ordinance of God's Church onely such as are regularly Caled and sent of God have been Ordained And Come under the hands of a Scriptural presbytry

4. The Church excluded Thomas Herrell from the fellowship of hur boddy on a Charge of Disorderly Conduct heare to fore taken And Caled Up this meeting

5. The Church took up a Charge against Sister Harrett Stephens for disorderly Conduct by Associating herself With persons of ill faim And Apointed Tildy Ricketts and Mary Stephens to inform hur of sd Charge

6. T. Stephens & Wife Wm A. F. Stephens and Wife aplied for Letters of Dismission Which Was Granted

Apointed McBride Clerk

Attest   S. M. Haun, Md.,
                                          Thos. Stephens, Clerk

SUNDAY AFTER THE 4TH SATURDAY IN SEPT. 1865

The Church met and adjorned from day to day until the following Sabbath in sd time transacted the following Buisness

Recvd by Exsperances G. I. Williams and his Wife Nancy Williams.

4TH SATURDAY OCTOBER

Church Met After preaching proceded to buisness

1st Opned a dore for the Reception of members Recvd by letter John D. Carter, Martin James by letter James G. Fortner by letter, George Snider by letter Catharine Snider letter Eliza Nucom by baptism, Herriet Newcom by baptism, Joseph Blakely by baptism.

4TH SAT. IN JANUARY.

Church Met After Worship proceded to Buisness

1st Opned a dore for the reception of members Recvd none.

2. A Charge taken Against Glen Renfro and excluded for drunkeness.

A charge taken against Bro. E. C. Herd for intoxication. Apointed Brothers McDaniel and J. Lane

4TH SAT. IN FEBRUARY

Church met and After Worship proceded to Buisness

1st Opned a dore for the Reception of members; Caled for the report of the Breathern in referance to Case reported, Excluded the brothers from the fellowship of the Church

P-103   4TH SATURDAY IN FEBURY 1865

Church met After Worship proceded to Buisness

1st Opned a dore for the Reception of members Recvd None.

2. the Church took up the Minutes of 64 Acted on And read the same.

4TH SATURDAY IN MARCH 1865

Church met After Worship proceded to buisness

1st opned a dore for the Reception of members Recvd None.

                                S. M. Haun, Md.
                                John McBride, Clk.

4TH SATURDAY IN APRILE 65

Church Met. After Worship proceded to buisness

1st Opened a dore for the Reception of members Recvd none Dismissed by letter Francis Shelton by letter Dismissed James Jarvis by letter.

                                S. M. Haun, Md.,
                                John McBride, Clk

4TH SATURDAY IN MARCH 66

Church Met and after Worship proceded to Buisness

1. Opned a dore for the reception of members. Recvd none Sabbath after preaching the Church Canled to order. Sister M. A. Cartrite handed back a letter to the Church Which she read 4th Saturday in September 1863

Done in Church conferance

S. M. Haun, Md.
John McBride, Clk

4TH SATURDAY IN APRIL.

Church met After Worship opned A dore for the reception of members. Recvd none. Brother Thomas Wallis Canled for a letter Which Was granted.

don in Church Conferans

S. M. Haun, Md.
John McBride, Clk

4TH SATURDAY IN MAY

Church Met After Worship proceded to buisness

1st Opned a dore for the reception of members. Recvd none

2. A petition from New Hopewell red and received the petition Canling for help to settle a difficulty in there Church. Appointed Breathern to Wit: George Stephens, Jacob Williams, Joseph Sands, George Jarvis And George Williams to Meet with the New Hopewell Church on the 2nd Saturday in Jun.

Don in Church Conferance. Signed by order of the Church.

S. M. Haun, Md.
John McBride, Clk.

P-104   4TH SATURDAY IN JUNE

Church Met. After Worship proceded to Buisness

1st Opned a dore for the Reception of members. Recvd none

4TH SAT. IN JULY

Church Met. After Worship proceded to buisness

1. Opned a dore for the reception of members. Recvd none

2. Appointed A protracted Meeting to Commence on Friday before the 4th Saturday in September, next

3. Apointed Breathern Samson Stephens, Elijah McDaniel and James

Hambrick to procure Ministerial And deacon Aid And Joseph Sands Also Apointed J. Sands and E. McDaniel deligates to the Association.

4TH SATURDAY IN AUGUST

Church Met After Worship proceed to business.

1. Opened a dore for the reception of members. Recvd Abraham Haun, and his Wife Ellen Haun by Letter Also James Hambrick by letter.

2. The letter to the Association Red and received

3. A Charge taken against Sister Matilda Blakeley for suing Brother S. Stephens unlawfully.

4. Apointed Brethern A. Haun & J. Hambrick to notify the sister of said Charge. this letter of Hambricks was given before the death of his Wife And handed to the Church after her death.

This don in Church Conferance 4 Saturday August 1866.

(In margin) Total number of members in the Church 173.

S. M. Haun, Mod.
John McBride, Clerk

4 SEPT.

Church met After Worship proceded to buisness

1. Opned a dore for the reception of members. Recvd none

2. Took up a charge against Sister Blakelay. She not being present laid over until next meeting.

3. A Charge taken Against John Stephens And Excluded for giting drunk and using profain language.

this don in Church Conferance.

S. M. Haun, Mod.
John McBride, Clk

Meeting Continued from day to day until Sabbath folowing. Recvd by expereans 1. Recvd by Baptism Caroline Hambrick

P-105   John McBride departed this Life in 1866

4TH SAT. IN OCTOBER

No meeting.

4TH SAT. IN NOVEMBER /66

Church met at Christianburg And After prar proceded to Buisness

1st Chose Brother A. Haun for the day as Moderator.

2nd Opened a dore for the reception of members. Recvd By Expriens Nancy Hitower

3rd Taken up a Reference Against Brother Thomas Emty And after some time he was Restored to the ful fellowship agane

4 the Church taken up a Referano Against Sister Matilda Blakly and after some Deliberation Excluded her from the fellowship of the Church

this done By order of the Church now in Conferano

A. Haun, Moderator
N. McDaniel, Clark protem

DECEMBER 4TH SATURDAY

Church met . No buisness done.

Sabith Morning met and After preaching proceded to Buisness

1. Opend a dore for the reCeption of members Recvd none.

Done by order of the Church now in Session

S. M. Haun, Mod.
A. McDaniel, Ac. Clerk

4TH SATURDAY IN JANUARY /67

Church met and after preaching proceded to buisness

1st Opened dore for the reception of members. Recvd none

2nd Sara Williams Caled for a letter of dismission which Was granted.

3rd George Williams and Nancy Williams Cald for leters of dismission Which Was granted

this done by order of the Church now in Session

S. M. Haun, Moderator
Elijah McDaniel, Clark protem

FEBRUARY 4TH SATURDAY

Church met. No preachin. Church Was Cald to order. Sister
Sara And Francis Harrill Cald for letters of dismission Which Was granted.

Sister Newcom departed the life   (P-106)   4th March

4 SATURDAY

Church Met And After Divine Worship proceded to bisness.

1st Brother Jeramarah Williams Cald for a letter of dismission Which Was granted.

2nd. Apointed Brother J. Sands house Comishner in the place of
Brother Thomas Stephens.

3rd. Recvd And Granted a petition from Big Springs Church Requestin us to send Brother J. Sands to Set in a Comity to help Setel a
Difficulty betwene G. Cate and E. Cate Which Was granted this done By
order of the Church now in Conferance. And also the Church altered her
meetin days from the 4 to the 2

E. McDaniel C. C. Protem

2ND SATURDAY IN APRILE /67

Church Met. No buisness transacted

E. McDaniel, C. Protem

2nd SATURDAY IN MAY /67

Church Met And After Divine Worship proceded to Buisness

1st Opend a dore for the Reception of members

2nd the Church Broat A Charge Against Sister Catharine Snider
for Ludeness And After hern the Evidence Excluded her from the fellowship
of the Church

E. McDaniel, C. C. Protem

Sister A. Carle Departed this Life May 23/67. Sister Sara Cunningham Departed this life June 9/67.

2ND SATURDAY JUNE /67

Church met And After Divine Worship procede to Bisness

1st Agreed to har a protracted Meatin to comenc on friday Before the 2 Saterday in October next And agreed to petition Cestee Chirch for Ministerial And Decan Aid And Brother Hightow bear the petition.

E. McDaniel, C. Protem

P-107   2ND SATURDAY IN JULY /67

Church Met And After Divine Worship proceded to Bisness

1st Opend a dore for the reception of members

2nd Ordered the Clark to Write the leter to the Sociation And hav it for inspection at the August meatin

3rd. Apointed Brother A. Hann J. Hightor And G. Stephens Delligats And in Case of falur S. Stephens, H. Cunningham And E. McDaniel to suply And Agread to send 3 dollars to help defray the Expence of the Asociation

this done By order of the Church now in Conferanc.

E. McDaniel, C. protem

2ND SATURDAY IN AUGUST /67

Church met And after Divine Worship procede to Bisness

1st Opend a dore for the Reception of members

E. McDaniel, C. Protem

2ND SATURDAY IN SEPTEMBER /67

Church Met And After Divine Worship proceded to Bisness

1st Taken up the Refferance of the Association leter the leter ben present it Was red and Recvd.

E. McDaniel, C. Protem
W. M. Haun, Md.

FRIDAY BEFOR THE 2ND SATURDAY IN OCTOBER

Church Met And After Devine Worship proceded to Bisness the metin Continued ten days in Which time the following bisness Was transacted Receiv Brother T. J. Nichols And his Wife Elizabeth Nichols By leter Recev Mary And Nancy J. Lane By experanc And Reciv Marraget Renfroe By Experanc And Reciv Moses Newcom By Experanc.   (P-108)   Reciv Sister Frances Sanders By Leter. Reciv Susan J. Longley By Experanc. Reciv Haner and Nancy Messor By Experanc. Reciv Husten Vance, Misouri Renfre, Nancy Cunningham, Marthy D. Williams, Charolote Lane, William McBroom, Orleane H. McBroom By Experranc Reciv a Boy of Culler By Experanc Sister Catharine Hambrick Cald for A leter of Dismission Which Was granted.

E. McDaniel, C. C. Protem

2ND SATURDAY IN NOVEMBER /67

Church met and After divine Worship proceded to Bisness

1st Opend A dore for the Reception of members And Reciv Nancy Stephens By Experanc

2nd Brother J. Hambrick Cald for a leter of dismission Which Was granted.

E. McDaniel, C. C. Protem

2ND SATURDAY IN DECEMBER /67

Church Met And after devine Worship proceded to Bisness

1st Opened a dore for the Reception of members

2nd Sister Hanner And Nancy Messors Cald for letters of dismission Which Was granted.

S. Haun Mod.
E. McDaniel, C. protem

2ND SATURDAY IN JANUARY /68

Church met and after divine Worship proceded to bisness

1st Opend a dore for the Reception of members

E. McDaniel, C. protem
S. M. Haun, Mod.

2ND SATURDAY IN FEBRUARY /68

Chirch Met And after Devine Worship proceded to Bisness

1st Opened a dore for the Reception of members.

E. McDaniel, C. Protem

P-109   Church met the Sunday After the 2nd Saturday in March. No Bisness done.

2ND SATURDAY IN APRILE /68

Church met and after Devine Worship proceded to Bisness

1st Opend a dore for the reception of members

2nd the Chirch Broat a Charge Against Brother Moses Newcom for Beyen good through falts pretente And Lien. It Ben lade over till next meten in Corse.

3rd the Chirch Broat a Charge Against Sister Lizy Newcom for Ludeness and excluded her upon the same

4th the Church broat A Charge Against Marry Newcom for liven in Adultres Sister not ben present the Church Apointed Sister Hightower And Sister Smith to notify her of the same

5th the Chirch broat a Charg Aganst Brother Robert Harrill for disorderly conduct and Exolude him from the fellowship of the Ohirch.

Reciv a patition from New Zion Chirch Requestin Christianburg to send her paster to atend them on the 1st Saturday in May next Which Was granted

this done By order of the Chirch in Conferrance.

E. McDaniel C. protem
S. M. Haun, Mod.

P-110   2ND SATURDAY IN MAY /68

Church Met and after Divine Worship proceded to Bisness

1st Opened a dore for the reception of members Reciv none

2nd the Church taken up the Referance from last meten Against Brother Moses Newcom. Brother Moses Ben present he gave satisfaction to the Church and the church forgav him

3rd then taken up the Refference Against Sister Mary Newcom
Sister Marry not Ben present it Was lade over until next meten in Corse

this done By Order of this Chirch now in Conferanc.

E. McDaniel, C. protem
S. M. Haun, Mod.

2ND SATURDAY IN JUNE /68

Chirch met and after Devine Worship proceded to Bisness

1st Opened a dore for the reception of members And Reciv Sister
Sara Fortner By leter

2nd Caled up the Referenc from last meetin Aganst Sister Mary
Newcom. Sister Marry not ben present it Was Continued til next meten
in Corst

this done by order of the Church now in Conferrance.

E. McDaniel, C. pro
S. M. Haun, Md.

3RD SATURDAY IN JULY /68

Chirch Met And After Divine Worship proceded to Bisness

1st Cald for the Refferance from last meten Aganst Sister Marry
Newcom. Sister Marry Ben present she satisfied the Church And the Church
forgiv her

2nd the Church Agread to har a sacremental meetin to Commence
on friday before the second Saturday in October.

P-111   3rd the Church Apeinted ther delligates to the Associations
to Wit Elder A. Haun, J. Sands and E. McDaniel And in Case of failure S.
Stephens and Wm B. Sampels Alternx And Agread to send up 2 dollars to
help defray the expenses of the Association

4th Reciv And granted a petition from New Zion Church requestin
the Church and officers to atend them on the 4 Saterday in August

5th the Church Broat A Charge aganst Sister Jane Burnet for
Ludeness and on sade Charge Excluded her from the fellowship of the Church

this done by order of the Church now in Conferanc.

E. McDaniel, C. C. &c.

2ND SATURDAY IN AUGUST /68

Church Met And After devine Worship proceded to Bisness

1st Cald for referance the leter ben broat forred red and recvd then adjorned to the time and place above named.

E. McDaniel, C. C. &c

SEPTEMBER

No meeting

2ND SATURDAY IN OCTOBER /68

Church Met And After Devine Worship proceded to Bisness

1st Opened a dore for the Reception of members Reciv Sister Elizabeth West and Sarah West by leter also Reciv Joseph Duncan by leter. Recvd Sister Rebeca Coil By Baptism

3rd Sisters Nancy Renfrow And Margret Renfrow And Misouri Renfrow Caled for leters of Dismission Which was granted

this done By order of the Church now in Conferance.

E. McDaniel, C. Clark

NOVEMBER.

No meeting.

P-112   2ND SATURDAY IN DECEMBER 1868

Church met And after Devine Worship proceded to buisness

1st Brother Elder A. Haun and Sister Elen Haun, his Wife, Caled for Leters of dismission Which Was granted.

2nd Brother Georg Snider Cald for a Leter of dismission Which Was granted

3rd Sister Marthy Hurd Cald for a Leter of dismission Which Was granted this done By order of the Church Now in Conferenc.

The church Apointed E. McDaniel Church Clark

E. McDaniel, C. C.

2ND SATURDAY IN JANUARY

No Meeting

2ND SATURDAY IN FEBRUARY /69

the Church Met And After Divine Worship proceded to Bissness

1st opened a dore for the reception of members. Recvd none

2nd Broat a Charge Against Sister Susan Ingram for Dancing And excluded her apon the same.

3rd Broat a Charge aganst Sister Orland H. McBroom for dancing And Excluded her apon the same

4th Also the Church broat a Charge Aganst Brother Levie Newcom for Drunkness And Apointed Breathern John Hightower And Davy Newcom to notify him of the same. Also broat a Charge Aganst Brother Moses Newcom for swaring And Apointed Brother Samson Stephens And Samuel Thomas to notify him of the same.

5th Brother John Fergerson And his Wife Catherine Fergerson Asked for Leters of dismission Which Was granted.

this done By order of the Church now in Conferanc.

E. McDaniel, C. R.

P-113   2ND SATERDAY IN MARCH /69

Church Met And after Devine Worship procede to Bisness

1st Opend a dore for the Reception of members. Recvd none

2nd Cald for the Refference Aganst Brother Levi Newcom. Brother Levi Ben present Mad acnoledgment And the Church forgiv him

3rd the Church taken up the Refference aganst Brother Moses Newcom. Brother Moses Ben present he did not giv satisfaction to the Church and the Church giv him the next meetin in Corse And the Church Apointed Sister Rebeca Coil to site Sister E. Smith and Sister Polly Hightower to site Sister Perky to appear as Witness Aganst him

this done By order of the Church now in Conferanc.

E. McDaniel C. P.
S. M. Haun, Md.

2ND SATURDAY IN APRILE /69

Church Met and after Devine Worship opned a dore for the Reception of members. Reciv Nancy M. Chrismen And Saraw R. J. Chrismon And J. A. Chrismon By Experanc.

2nd Taken up the refferenc from last meaten aganst Brother Moses Newcom. Brother Moses not ben present the Church declared an unfellowship aganst him

3rd the Church agread to ancer the quary in May from the Association the propriety or impropriety of Consolidating the two Sweetwater Associations and Apointing of Mishionary.

this done By order of the Church now in Conference.

E. McDaniel, Clk.
S. M. Haun, Md.

P-114   2ND SATURDAY IN MAY /69

Church Met And After Worship proceded to bisness

1st Opend a dofe for the reception of members. Reciv none

2nd In Ancer to the Quarys the Church is in favor of a Consolidation of the two Sweetwater Associations As it is laid down in the Minnet of 65

3rd the Magarety of the Church is Aposed to Apointing Mishonary. Sabith After Worship open a dore for the reception of members and Reciv Sister Hanah C. Rowan by letter

4th Brother T. J. Nichols And his Wife Elizabeth Nichols aplise for leters of dismission Which Wes granted

this By order of the Church now in Conferance

E. McDaniel, Clk

2ND SATURDAY IN JUNE /69

Church met and after Devine Worship - No bisness done.

E. McDaniel, C. K.
S. M. Haun, Md.

2ND SATERDAY IN JULY /69

Church Met And after Devine Worship proceded to Bisness

1st Opened a dore for the Reception of members and Reciv by
Leter Brother Isaac Chrismon and his Wife Sara Chrismon

this done By order of the Church now in Conferenc.

E. McDaniel, C. K.
S. M. Haun, Md.

2ND SATERDAY IN AUGUST /69

Church met and After Devine Worship proceded to bisness

1st Opend a dore for the Reception of members. Reciv none

2nd the Church apointed her delligates to the Association to
Meat With the Rodgers Creek Church on friday before the third Saturday in
September next (P-115) to Wit Elijah McDaniel, Wm B. Sampel, and Sampson
Stephens and the Church Agrease to send up two dollars to help defray the
Expenses of the Association

3rd the Curch order the Clark to Write a leter to the Association And hav it for inspection next meatin.

4th Sister Charity Sheats Aplise for a leter of dismission
Which Was granted.

5th. Sisters Elizabeth West And Sarah West aplise for leters
of dismission Which Was granted.

S. M. Haun, Mod.
E. McDaniel, C. K.

2ND SATERDAY IN SEPTEMBER 1869

Church met And after Devine Worship proceded to Bisness

1st Opend a dore for the reception of members and reciv by Experance Nathaniel Thomas

2nd   Brother Joseph Dunken aplied for a leter of dismission Which Was granted.

3rd   Sister M. E. Snider aplise for a leter of dismission Which Was Granted.

S. M. Haun Mod.
E. McDaniel, Clerk

2ND SATERDAY IN OCTOBER 1869

Church met and after Devine Worship proceded to Bisness

1st   Opend a Dore for the Reception of members and reciv By leter Brother Elijah Sims

2nd   Sister Nancy Lane E. Newcom And Howard Newcom his Wife Aplide for leters of dismission Which Was granted

3rd   Henry Walker Collard aplide for a leter of dismission Which Was granted.

4th   Moses Newcom joined by enrollment

Reciv By Leter Brother John Gallaher Reciv By Leter Brother John Swagety. Reciv By Leter Sister Carroline Russell

this done in Church Conferran

S. M. Haun, Mod.
E. McDaniel, Clk

P-116   2ND SATURDAY IN NOVEMBER /69

Church met And after Devine Worship proceded to bisness

1st   Opend a dore for the reception of members and reciv by baptism Catharine McBroom and Susan McBroom And Aaron Harrill and dismist by Leter Lemuel Newcom then Adjurned to the time and plase above named.

S. M. Haun, Clk.
E. McDaniel, Md.

(In margin) The Church Liberated Brother G. J. Fortner to ex- ercise his Gift in the bouns of the Church

2ND SATURDAY IN DECEMBER /69

Church met and after devine Worship proceded to bisness

1st. Opned a dore for the reception of members. Reciv none

2nd the Minit from the Association of 67 Was red and reciv By the Church

this done in Church Conferranc.

S. M. Haun, Mod.
E. McDaniel, Clk

2ND SATERDAY IN JANUARY /70

Church Met And after Devine worship proceded to bisness

1st Opend a doar for the Reception of members And Reciv By Experanc July Hightower And Susan Hicks

2nd Granted a Leter of Dismission to Brother T. Hunt

this done in Church Conferranc the day an dat abov Writen.

S. M. Haun, Mod.
E. McDaniel, Clk

2ND SATERDAY IN FEBUARY /70

Church Met And After Devine Worship preseded to Bisness

1st Opened a dore for the Reception of members reciv None.
No other bisness transacted.

S. M. Haun, Mod.
E. McDaniel, Clk

James Weathers departed this Life in Calafoind

P-117   2ND SATURDAY IN MARCH /70

Church Met and after Devine Worship proceded to bisness

1st Opened a dore for the reception of members. Reciv None

S. M. Haun, Mod.
F. McDaniel, Clk

2ND SATERDAY IN APRILE 1870

Church Met and After Devine Worship proceded to Bisness

1st Opend a dore for the Reception of members   Reciv. None

E. McDaniel, Clk

2ND SATURDAY IN MAY /70

Church Met and After Devine Worship proceded to Bissness

1st Opend a dore for the reception of members

2nd Apointed A Comite to tri to setel a difficulty Between Brother Huse and his Wife Nancy Huse to Wit John Hightower, A. Harrill An Samson Stephens An report at the next meating in Corse

this done in Church Conferen By order of the Church the day and date Abov Written.

E. McDaniel, Clk

2ND SATERDAY IN JUNE /70

Church Met and after Devine Worship proceded to Bisness

1st Opend a dore for the Reception of members   the Comite Apointed last Reported and Nothing mor done with it

this done By order of the Church the day an date abov Writen.

E. McDaniel, Clk.
S. M. Haun, Mod.

P-118   2ND SATERDAY IN JULY 1870

Church Met And After Devine Worship proceded to Bissness

1st Opend a dore for the Reception of members. Reciv none

S. M. Haun, Mod.
E. McDaniel, Clk

2ND SATERDAY IN AUGUST /70

Church Met and after Devine Worship proceded to Bissness

1st Opend a dore for the Reception of members. Reciv Non
2nd The Church Apointed ther Delligates to the Association

to viz. Joseph Sands, Elijah McDaniel An Wm B. Sampels

3rd the Church Agread to send up two dollars to help pay the expences of the Association

4th Order the Clark to Wright the Leter to the Association And hav it at Nex Meaten for inspection. then Adjurned

S. M. Haun, Mod.
E. McDaniel, Church C.

2ND SATERDAY IN SEPTEMBER 1870

Church met and After Devine Worship proceded to Bissness

1st Opend a dore for the Reception of members Reciv. None

2nd Cald for the Leter to the Association the Leter Was red an reciv

3rd the Church Agread to hav a sacremental meating to Comence on Friday before the Second Saterday in November next then ajurned.

S. M. Haun, Mod.
E. McDaniel, Clk

2ND SATERDAY IN OCTOBER.

No meeting

P-119   2ND SATERDAY IN NOVEMBER

Church Met And After Devine Worship proceded to Business

1st Opend a dore for the Reception of members

2nd Brother Samson Stephens an Elizabeth Stephens his Wife Rebeca Stephens, his daughter Margret Stephens, his daughter and sister Nancy Thomas aplide for Leters of Dismission Which Was granted

this done in Church Conferrence the day and date above Writen.

S. M. Haun, Mod.
E. McDaniel, Ck.

2ND SATERDAY IN DECEMBER

Church met and after Devine Worship proceded to Bissness

Church met and after Devine worship proceded to Bissness

1st Opend a dore for the Reception of members

2nd Taken a charg Against Brother Levi Newcom for Drunkness an excluded him from the fellowship of the Church

3rd taken a charg aganst Brother Sanders for Drunkness and Apointed Brother John Hightower an Brother James Forkner to sight him to atend next meating in cors.

4th taken a charg aganst Brother Elijah Simes for Drunkness and Apointed Brother Joseph Sands to Wright to him to extend and giv satisfaxion to the Church the meating continued 10 days in Which time the following Bisness was transacted.

5th Reciv by Experanc William Stephens, Levi Newcom, Edmon Delosure, Marry Snead, Susan Sneed, Sidney Snead, Mirry Snead, Caroline Harress, Carroline Smith, Marten McBrosm

S. M. Haun, Mod.
E. McDaniel Clk

P-120   2ND SATERDAY IN JANUARY 1871

Church met and after Devine Worship proceded to Bisness

1st Opend a dore for the reception of members and Reciv Brother E. Z. Haris and Saline Haris his wife By Letter

2nd Cald for the Referance from last meeting Brother Sanders bean present Made acnolegments and the Church forgiv himm Also Brother Simes bean present made acnolegments and the Church forgiv him. Also granted Brother Elijah Simes A letter of dismission.

S. M. Haun, Mod.
E. McDaniel, Clk

2ND SATERDAY IN FEBUARY 1871

Church met and after Worship proceded to Bisness

1st opened a dore for the Reception of Members

2nd taken a charge Aganst Brother Moses Newcom for swaren And Apointed Brethern to notify him of the same to viz: Brother J. Sands, G. Coile and E. McDaniel then ajurned

S. M. Haun, Mod.
E. McDaniel, Clk

2ND SATERDAY IN MARCH 1871

Church Met And after Worship proceded to Besness

1st opened a dore for the Reception of members

2nd taken up the Reference from last meaten aganst Brother Moses Newcom And Excluded him apon the same, then ajurned

S. M. Haun, Mod.
E. McDaniel, C. Clk

2ND SATERDAY IN APRILE

Church Met an After Worship proceded to Bisness

1st Reciv an granted a petition from Union, McMinn Church requesting of us our paster an Deacons aid to asist them at a Sacremental Meeting to Commence on (P-12) Friday before the first Saterday in May nex

done by order of the Church now in session. No other Bisness transacted.

S. M. Haun, Mod.
E. McDaniel, C.K.

2ND SATERDAY IN MAY

Church met and after Divine Worship proceded to Bissness

1st Opend a dore for the Reception of members and Reciv Joseph Forkner By Baptism

S. M. Haun, Mod.
E. McDaniel, C. R.

2ND SATERDAY IN JUNE

Church Met and after worship proceded to Bissness

1st opend a dore for the Reception of members. Reciv One

2nd Granted a Leter of dismission to Elizabeth Williams

S. M. Haun, Mod.
E. McDaniel, C. R.

2ND SATERDAY IN JULY

Church met and after worship proceded to Bissness

1st Opend a dore for the Reception of members Reciv none

2nd Reciv an granted a patishion from Youing, McMinn Church Requested this Church ther Ministerial And Deacon aid to atend them at a sacremental meting to Commence on Friday before the first Saterday in September next

this done by order of the Church Now in Conferance.

S. M. Haun, Mod.
E. McDaniel, C. R.

P-122   2ND SATERDAY IN AUGUST 1871

Church met And After Devine Worship proceded to Busness first Chosen Brother James Forkner Moderator for the day

2nd opend a dore for the Reception of members Reciv none

3rd the Church Apointed there Dellightes to the Association to viz Elders James Farkner, H. Cunningham, An L. Crismor an Order the Clark to Wright the Leter an hav it for inspection at our next Meeting.

4th Agread to send 2 dollars to help defray the Expence of the Association the Church Agrees to hav A Sacremental Meating to Commeno on Friday beforre the second Saterday in October an we potishion Union, Mc-Minn an County line Churches for ther Minerstral An Deacons Aid

done in Church Conferens the day an date above reten.

S. M. Haun, Mod.
E. McDaniel, C. Clark

2ND SATERDAY IN OCTOBER

Church Met And After prar proceded to Bisness

1st opend a dore for the Reception of members

2nd Sister Polly Ann Peterson Aplide for a Leter of dismission Which was granted

done by Order of the Church in Conferrance

E. McDaniel, C. Clark
S. M. Haun, Mod.

P-123   2ND SATERDAY IN NOVEMBER

Church met and after Worship proceded to Bisness

1st   Opend a dore for the Reception of members and Recivd the
folowin persons By Baptism:

                         John Renfroe
                         Robert A. McDaniel
                         James Stephens
                         Thomas G. Harris
                         Sally E. Harris

By Experience

                         Francis P. Sampels

Octavy Brennon

This done in Church Conferance the day And date abov riten.

                  2ND SATERDAY IN DECEMBER

Church met and after Devine Worship proceded to Bissness

1st   Open a dore for the Reception of members

2nd   Brother Harison Davis And his Wife Elizabeth Davis Aplide
for Leters of dismission Which Was granted

done in Church Conferan.

                         E. McDaniel, C. R.
                         S. M. Haun, Mod.

                  2ND SATERDAY IN JANUARY 1872

Church met and after Worship opened a dore for the Reception of
members Reciv none. No other Bisness transacted.

                         E. McDaniel, C. R.
                         S. M. Haun, Mod.

                  2ND SATERDAY IN FEBUARY 1872

Church Met and after Worship proceded to Bissness

1st   taken a charge Aganst Sister Marry Purky for fornication
And excluded her from the fellowship of the Church

2nd   Sister Hannah Romans Aplide for a letter of dismission Which Was granted

3rd   the Church apointed a Comety to Get up a Corect list of our Churches to Wit

E. McDaniel
J. Sands
W. B. Sampels

then adjurned

S. M. Haun, Mod.
E. McDaniel, C.R.

P-124   2ND SATERDAY IN MARCH 1972

Church met and after Devine Worship proceded to Bissness

1st   Opend a dore for the Reception of Members   Reciv none

2nd   Brother John Newcom aplide for a Leter of Dismission Which Was granted

this done in Church Conferanc the day and dat abov writen

E. McDaniel, C. R.
S. M. Haun, Mod.

2ND SATERDAY IN APRILE 1872

Church met and after Devine Worship proceded to Bissness

1st   opend a dore for the Reception of members   Reciv None

2nd   Reciv an granted an patiahion from Union, McMin Church Requestin our paster and Deacons Aid to atend them on the firs Saterday and Sunday in May

done in Church Conferanc   then adjurned

2ND SATERDAY IN MAY 1872

Church Met an After Devine Worship proceded To Bisness

1st   Cald for the Report of the Comite that Was Apinted to git up a Corect List of the Church   the Comite Reported an the Report Was reciv an the Comite Discharg done in Church Conferenc the day an date abov Roten.

2ND SATERDAY IN JULY –

No Bisness done

P-125   2ND SATERDAY IN JUNE 1872

Church Met and after Worship proceded to Bissness

Opend A dore for the Reception of members.   Reciv None

2ND SATERDAY IN AUGUST 1872

Church met and after Worship proceded to Bisness

1st Apointed the Delligats to the Association to viz. E. F.
Hariss, J. Sands, and E. McDaniel, And in Case of fa uer A. Harrill An
H. Vance alternates And Agread to Contribute two dollars to help fray
the Expenc of the Asociation

2nd the Church Broat a Charg Against Brother Joseph Blakly for
swaring And excluded him apon the same

3rd Reciv an granted a potition from Union, McMin, Requestin
us our paster an Deacons to atend them on friday Before the first Saterday in September next

4th Reciv and granted a potition from County Line requestin
us our paster and decons to atend them at a Sacremental Meeting to Commenc
on Friday Before the third Saterday in August 1872 Also we agread to hav
a Sacremental Meating to Commence on friday Before the Secon Saterday in
October next and potition the folowin Church for Aid to viz. Union, Mc-
Min And Brother J. Chrismon Bars the potition County Line And Brother J.
Sands Bare potition Also Chestoe and Brother E. F. Hares bare the potition.

P-126   2ND SATERDAY IN SEPTEMBER /72

members.   Church Met And After Worship opened a dore for the Reception of
            Reciv None

granted   3rd William Stephens Cald for a Leter of dismission Which Was
            granted

Done by order of the Church the day And date Abov Writen.

                              E. McDaniel C. R.
                              S. M. Haun Md.

www.ingramcontent.com/pod-product-compliance
Lightning Source LLC
Chambersburg PA
CBHW080242270326
41926CB00020B/4346